EYES FULL OF SKY

Selected Works from the COMPAS
Writers & Artists in the Schools Program

Edited by
Stephen Peters

Illustrations by
Chloe DeJong Hilden

Writers & Artists in the Schools
2007

Publication of this book is generously supported by the Lillian Wright and C. Emil Berglund Foundation, dedicated in memory of C. Emil Berglund.

COMPAS programs are made possible in part by grants provided by the Minnesota State Arts Board, through an appropriation by the Minnesota State Legislature. Additional support has been provided by many generous corporations and foundations which can be found at our website www.compas.org/pages/artsedfunders.html.

As always, we are grateful for the hundreds of excellent teachers throughout Minnesota who sponsor COMPAS Writers & Artists in the Schools residencies. Without their support and hard work, the writers and artists would not weave their magic, and the student work we celebrate in this book would not spring to life.

Book Production: Betsy Mowry, WAITS Program Associate; and
                 Daniel Gabriel, Arts Education Programs Director

Book Design: Betsy Mowry

ISBN 0-927663-42-2

Illustrations ©2007 by Chloe DeJong Hilden
Illustrations photographed by Usry Alleyne
Music, Additional Words, Arrangements ©2007 by Charlie Maguire and Mello-Jamin Music
Text ©2007 COMPAS

COMPAS
75 Fifth Street West, Suite 304
Saint Paul, Minnesota 55102

Jeff Prauer, Executive Director
Daniel Gabriel, Arts Education Programs Director

EYES FULL OF SKY is dedicated to Ron Clark,
long-time Editorial Page Editor at the *Saint Paul Pioneer Press*, who, as a Board member of COMPAS and a community leader, tirelessly committed himself to furthering opportunities for creative self-expression.

TABLE OF CONTENTS

THE TREE OF MAGICAL COOKIES

DEAR NATURE

MOMENTS NOT TO BE FORGOTTEN

INTRODUCTION

If someone had told me twenty-some years ago that I would be editing anthologies of writing by young people and spending most of every school year visiting schools to teach writing—year after year, joyfully—I would have laughed out loud. I had been teaching university courses back then and planned to do that and write for the rest of my career. Elementary and high school teaching? No way.

But somehow—and I won't bother to tell that story—I ended up on the COMPAS roster of writers and artists, at first thinking this would be temporary, a lark. Now all those years and all that hair loss later, here I am, happily telling you about my delight at doing this work.

Why delight? Read *Eyes Full of Sky* and you will know. You have to love the children and young adults in these pages. They will tell you of their dreams and sorrows, of their whimsy and fantasy. They will touch your heart, and they will make you laugh. This is a ride through sunny and cloudy moods, through the origins and influences that shape us, through pure, imaginative fun, through the natural world, and through those pivotal moments that change us forever.

The chapter "Weathered Feelings," a title gleaned from Franchesca Castro's poem, gets us started. Sometimes, she writes, she is "bright and sunny . . . Other days I feel cloudy . . ." The ups and the downs, in other words. You'll find both in this chapter. The silly fun of "The Squeak Came Back," by Janelle Bute and Piper Day, must have been a sunny day! And Muhammad Ali step aside. Daniel Johnson's sunny rap may not be about boxing, but we can hear Ali's voice rocking right through the rhymes of "Basketball Rap," chest-thumping bravado worthy of the Greatest. The chapter is an introduction to the array of moods that will recur through the rest of the anthology.

"Five Lanes of Destiny," the second chapter, explores the influences that make us what and who we are, celebrating the diversity of our experiences and origins—both national and personal. Jaylin Stroot's "My Town" evokes the warmth of the close-knit community so much a part of the traditional American small town. "The slow rumble of the cars/As they glide down the avenues/Is a sweet lullaby/Playing for all who need to rest." We see the diversity of our national community when we set these images next to Fadli Mohamed's "Home," a searching meditation on what "home" really means. The conclusion Fadli comes to tells the story of countless immigrants over the centuries as they assimilate into and enrich American culture. This spirit is nicely captured in "Immigration From Every Nation," by the fourth graders at North Intermediate School, who also give the title to this chapter. And Anna Lucia Krupp's beautiful reflections on who she is and how she fits give this anthology its title.

While "Five Lanes of Destiny" points to the life experience molding these young writers, "The Tree of Magical Cookies," from Hailey Pietraszewaski's story of that name, takes us in a completely different direction. Now we are in the realm of pure imagination and fun. You'll find some truly strange stuff here. Devin Kelly's so, so clever "Unexpected Aliens" will have you scratching your head and practicing your backwards spelling, then cracking up at his zaniness. Second grader Amelia Broman retells the Pegasus myth in her own unique way, and Katie Hoff's "In the Stomach of . . ." will send your imagination to a dark and rather hilarious place. Not to be missed is Chris Murphy's "The Elf of Terabal," an impressively mature piece of fourth grade writing.

"Dear Nature," the shortest chapter in the book, occupies a special place in my heart. In an age of computer games and ubiquitous television sets, these visits to natural places and interactions with animals and individual trees and swamps and woods ground the anthology. Many, many of us, I'm sure, have felt, and maybe longed for, the consoling wonder of natural phenomena, as in Madeline Hudalla's "Dear Cloud," which tells of being comforted by looking at clouds when she feels homesick. Many of the pieces—Kellie Metzger's "The Importance of Our Pine Tree" and Samantha Abbott's "The Swan Who Followed Samantha," to name just two—took me back to my boyhood playing in Pennsylvania's barns and woods and along the banks of the Delaware River. Perhaps more than any other, this is a timeless chapter.

These moments in nature change and deepen us; the experiences in "Moments Not to be Forgotten" have a similar impact. They indelibly mark the young writers in this chapter. After the experience in Michelle Atwood's "Talent Show," she will always be a performer. The tragic loss of a sibling, as in Do-Hyoung Park's piece, "Life Goes On," or the Zen moment of watching the grass shiver in Forrest Ahern's poem, will leave the writers changed. Special notice should be given to Liz Massie's "A Favor for Papa," a truly touching story of a girl being given a responsibility that marks her coming of age in her family.

While choosing the stories and poems and songs for *Eyes Full of Sky*, I kept wondering how, years from now, the young writers in these pages would react to rereading their words. Other writers and I have talked about the experience of returning to a piece of published work after having not seen it for a long, long time. It is sometimes a shock, as if some stranger had written the words and then put our names on them.

"Did *I* write that?" we wonder. "Where did that idea come from? Did *I* turn that clever phrase?"

And so I wonder if these young authors will some day ask themselves these same questions. I hope they do. I hope they are as amazed by the wisdom and wordplay and, for many of them, the nutty, entertaining fun that has given me, their editor, genuine pleasure and wonder. I hope they do, and I wish, impossibly, that I could be standing next to each one of them for that magical moment.

"Yes," I would say. "You did write that. You did turn that clever phrase. Now write more."

Stephen Peters

A Note to Teachers Using
Eyes Full of Sky with your students
by Stephen Peters

The editor of last year's anthology, Julia Klatt Singer, said it best: "Put this book on your desk or on a shelf where both you and your students can stumble across it often." Indeed, this book, like the COMPAS anthologies from other years, would be a happy addition to your classroom bookshelf or literature carousel. Ideally, it would always be within easy reach, as both a reminder of what students left to their own imaginations can create and a collection of examples for you and your students to draw on. Whether your lesson is about rap, memoir, fantasy, humor, realistic fiction, free verse, dramatic structure, characterization, simile, metaphor, or how to punctuate dialogue, your students will find plenty of examples to learn from in these pages.

The reluctant students in your class may be inspired by the work of students their own age. "So you don't have to be a professional sitting on a throne on a mountaintop to write a story or poem," is the feeling these students might have. "This author is a fourth grader, just like I am. I wonder . . . " Suddenly the student is scribbling out words from an imaginative place he didn't know he had. And your more confident students may be inspired to outdo what they find here. Both are excellent and not-at-all-unheard-of reactions to the COMPAS anthologies. Not only are kids likely to be entertained by what their peers have written, but they will recognize the experiences and sensibilities of other young writers. "Ah, so I can really write about the funeral of my grandfather. Since there is such a memoir here in this anthology, I obviously do have permission to relive that sad day on paper and I might even find some good in doing so." Doors open when kids read what other kids have written.

And the COMPAS anthologies serve as bridges. They can be bridges to classroom writing assignments: Write about what would happen if aliens suddenly landed in your back yard. Write about what it would be like to be swallowed by an animal. Write a memory of when your family gave you a special responsibility. The anthologies are also bridges to other literature. Your discussions about the work you find in *Eyes Full of Sky* can lead into discussing and then reading through the wealth of professional literature available in your class-room and media center. How are the adventure stories found in the COMPAS anthologies like or different from adventures such as Gary Paulson's *Hatchet*? We model much of what we do on the work of others, standing on the shoulders of writers who have come before us. What have your students read that they can relate to this story or poem in the anthology? What are the literary influences inspiring the work in the anthology? Your class could read Chris Murphy's "The Elf of Terabal," for example, and then discuss, in addition to what's going on in the story, what adult writers Chris must be reading.

The best use of the anthology, though, is to know it well enough yourself that you can lead individual students to particular pieces. Teachers know what is going on in the lives of their students. They know which children love horses or basketball or fantasy. You name it. They also know which students are going through difficult times at home and so can lead students to stories or poems that may make them feel less alone. Teachers, you can give a page or so of reading as a special gift—with absolutely no other agenda than to recognize that one student's individual personality.

I Remember

I remember when I was carefree in the
world, running around with the wind
messing up my hair.
I remember when I didn't have to
worry about what people thought of me—
my hair, the way I dressed, my attitude.
I remember when I could eat whatever
I wanted and knew I would burn
it off.
I remember when we had an old oak
tree in our yard that would look down
at me. Too bad that tree is gone now
it was my favorite.
I remember when I would actually
choose favorite trees.
I remember when our ugly gray car
brought us places no one knew it could.
I remember when I realized the game
LIFE was only slightly like real life.

Elizabeth Rigstad
Grade 9
Roseau Secondary School, Roseau
Writer-in-residence: John Minczeski

Weathered Feelings

Inside I am like weather.
Some days
bright and sunny,
ready to
jump
for
joy
at the thought of life.
Other days I feel cloudy
just to the point of a
thunderstorm
of
rage.
I also get
hurricanes
of
      hate
        and
   tornados
     of
trouble
sucking me into the depths
of anger. . .
Then my eyes
get all misty, the
tears
rolling
down
my
cheeks
the way rain rolls down
car windows,
floods of sadness
drowning me
to the point of death.
So my only hope
is for the
    sun to shine
     again,

drying the floods
    around me
so I
can breathe
once again.

Franchesca Castro
Grade 5
Alice Smith Elementary School, Hopkins
Writer-in-residence: Joyce Sidman

Spell for a Bad Day

Be the victim of a dog's morning
breath as a wake up call.
Be the style horror of the
day—two socks but no match.
Be the first to walk out and
smell the crisp taste
of global warming.
Be the victim of a moldy
raw donut you throw
out your window, hitting
a police car.
Be the one to run from
the high speed chase.
Be the one whose
computer breaks down
while your presentation's already
a day late. Be the one
to have a smile through it all.

Rajanae Whitmore
Grade 5
Gatewood Elementary School, Hopkins
Writer-in-residence: John Minczeski

The Squeak Came Back
(Melody: "The Cat Came Back")

I went down to the hardware store
To get some oil for my old squeaky door
I slipped and fell on the wet ground
I found myself slippin' all around.

CHORUS: But the squeak came back the very next day
The squeak came back
I thought it was a goner
But the squeak came back
It just wouldn't stay away.

Now my squeaky problem is solved
Just as my best friend called
But then I heard a squeak through the house
The squeaking sound came from a mouse.
CHORUS

I saw the fuzzy mouse sitting on the ground
So I started to chase him all around

(spoken)
He goes around the couch and the chair!
He slips around one corner, then the other
And into the mouse hole, near the old squeaky door.
The mouse wins!

CHORUS: But the squeak came back the very next day
The squeak came back
I thought it was a goner
But the squeak came back
It just wouldn't stay away.

(spoken): Squeak!

Janelle Bute and Piper Day
Grade 6
St. Joseph's School, West Saint Paul
Musician-in-residence: Rachel Nelson

It was Like a Vacation

Chapter 1: Tired Jim

My name is Claude Daniels and the story that I'm about to tell you is about something I like to call a vacation. It all started about two months ago when I was going to school with my best friend Jim Taylors.

"Hey Jim," I said as I ran down my front steps. Jim had stopped walking and he was staring at me real hard like I was invisible or something. I was about to ask him if he was okay, when he started to sway back and forth. I was looking at him with wide eyes when he seemed to lean too far and was thrown off balance. Then he went tumbling to the ground.

I ran over and picked him up and asked, "What's wrong?"

"Oh, I'm just tired," he answered.

"Okay," I said as I walked back up the steps to grab my backpack.

Chapter 2: School's Out

When we got to school, the first thing we noticed was that all the lights weren't on. Then we heard a familiar voice. It was our friend Carol.

"Hey, what are you guys doing here?" She asked as she walked over to us.

"What are we . . . what are you doing here?" I asked as I walked closer to her.

"Well, I know what I was coming here to do," Carol exclaimed. "I was coming here to learn why school is out."

"What . . . school is out?" Jim and me asked together.

"Yeah, school's out. There aren't any lights on and nobody's here but us," Carol explained.

I peeked in the third grade pod. "Nobody in here," I said as I pulled my head out of the door. But Carol and Jim weren't there.

Chapter 3: Runaway Teachers

I was searching for Jim and Carol when I noticed a light in the teachers' lounge. Then I heard voices. It was Jim and Carol. I lifted the lounge door open and stepped in. Jim and Carol were leaning over a small round table. They were looking at something but I couldn't tell what it was. Then they turned and looked at me and motioned for me to come closer. So I did and to my surprise sitting on the table was a note from our principal.

> To whoever is reading this. The teachers and I have gone on a vacation to Hawaii and wont be back for some time.
> So we have shut down the school until we come back.
>   Sincerely,
>   Ms. Petta

"Well, I guess we're not going to be going to school for a while," Carol said. We were walking home from school and Carol was very disappointed about school being closed. "No more being excited when the bell rings for recess," she said dramatically.

"I think you're overreacting," Jim said.

"Humph," Carol said and stomped ahead.

"Well, I thought that letter was strange," I said. "First, it didn't look a thing like Ms. Petta's handwriting, and second, Ms. Petta wouldn't write *to whoever is reading this* and *until we come back*. She would write, *to whom it may concern* and *until we return*. But of course, I could be wrong."

So we walked home and got an extra long . . . vacation.

The End . . . or, is it?

Serena Minnihan
Grade 4
Gatewood Elementary School, Hopkins
Writer-in-residence: Stephen Peters

I Never Knew

I never knew I liked
taking a shower
after a long day
the water pouring out of the faucet
like warm rain in broad daylight

I never knew I liked
vacuuming the floors
the sound of the *virr* . . . coming
from the vacuum
sucking up dust mites to grubby paper
I push along the ground
as if nothing could stand in my way

And I sit here on my bed
watching the twinkling stars
my toys my companions
the red light of my alarm clock reads 7:12
the time of night
the time when moon awakens
from its slumber
I never knew I liked the night

Some are wise like a whale
some are curious like a kitten
but I never knew I liked the mind
smarter than a super computer
unknown to the unknown

I never knew
I liked so many things
and a good thing too
because hate is a strong word
and sometimes
I don't know my own strengths.

Kaley Inman
Grade 5
Tanglen Elementary School, Hopkins
Writer-in-residence: John Minczeski

Cute Shoes

I'm sorry that I took your shoes
that day I went to the party.

I'm sorry you couldn't find them
when you went looking in your closet.

I'm sorry I scuffed them
when I almost fell.

I'm sorry they were cute
and fit pretty well.

I'm sorry the heels were just the right size,
and I had just gotten a pedicure
so my toes caught your eyes.

Last but not least, I'm sorry
because they looked so cute on me.

Yahrielle Shavers
Grade 4
Liberty Ridge Elementary School, Woodbury
Writer-in-residence: Joyce Sidman

Brownies

I'm sorry I ate the brownies . . .
Yes, I knew they were for your boss,
but they were just so tempting.
When I was calling you to ask if I could have them,
I got another call. I knew who it was from.
The brownies . . . they were calling me. So!
I went over and searched the gooey plate
for the biggest, most chocolaty brownie,
When I found it, I had a bite or two,
or three, or eighty-seven. But I couldn't stop after that.
I had another and another . . .
till I reached down and there were no more!
So, I'm sorry I ate
the most delicious brownies in the world
that were for your boss . . .
but I couldn't help it.

Kyle Nelson
Grade 5
Royal Oaks Elementary School, Woodbury
Writer-in-Residence: Joyce Sidman

The Way Around Detention

"Bob, wake up or it's detention!" yelled Miss Fur.

Bob woke with a start. "Yes, Miss Fur."

"So, Bob, tell me what the answer is."

Bob looked up at the blackboard (94 x 89). "Ah, the answer is, um, ah, five-hundred something?"

Miss Fur looked at Bob like he was a snake. (Miss Fur hated snakes.) "No, Bob. The answer isn't five-hundred something."

The rest of the class sniggered. Susan put her fist in her mouth to stop from laughing out loud. Dean, on the other side of the room, threw a piece of paper to Bob when Miss Fur wasn't looking. "Open it," he mouthed. Bob opened it. *You are stupid*, it said over and over again.

"I'M NOT STUPID!" Bob thundered over the class.

"Bob!" yelled Miss Fur. "Detention!"

"What?"

"You heard me, Bob. Detention, buster! Class dismissed," Miss Fur barked.

"Hey, Bob, you are stupid, aren't you?" Dean said, without troubling to keep his voice down.

"Dean!"

"What?"

"Detention for both you and Bob," said Miss Fur.

"What for?" Dean turned red.

Bob whispered, "You are stupid, aren't you?"

"You two will do your detention together right now. Write 'I will not disturb the class' five hundred times with your pencil. Begin!" Then she left the room.

"See you later," Dean said. Then he opened the window and jumped out for recess. Bob had written 'I will not disturb the class' only twice when he went out the window to stop Dean. Just then Miss Fur stepped into the room.

"What do you think you're doing?" yelled Miss Fur.

"Dean jumped out the window, Miss Fur," Bob said.

Dean entered the room and said, "Nice, refreshing drink."

Miss Fur looked at Bob and said, "Double detention for telling such lies, Bob. Come with me!"

Bob followed her out the door as Dean gave him a nasty look.

"Come on!" yelled Miss Fur. She led him straight to Mr. Zan, the principal. "Go!" said Miss Fur. Then she turned and faced Mr. Zan.

"Bob was given detention and tried to climb out the window."

They left him alone in the room to go talk over his punishment. Bob noticed an air vent. He climbed up to it, crawled inside, and came out the other side of the school. He was free and had not gotten expelled.

Nolan Bach
Grade 4
Hilltop Elementary School, Henderson
Writer-in-Residence: Stephen Peters

Escape to School

Principal's Office. The words were familiar. Yet every time Carl Lynford saw them he grimaced. Carl wasn't a bully, or a class clown. He was just ordinary. Then why was he in the principal's office? People say things that aren't true, you know. . . .

The door opened. "Carl Lynford," Mr. Burns boomed. Mr. Burns liked to pretend to be official. When the secretary, Mrs. Brown, had a phone call, Mr. Burns would make her say, "Please hold," so it sounded busy.

"I've seen you a lot lately." He spun back and forth in his chair mockingly.

"And what did I do now?" asked Carl. That's a weird thing for someone to say, unless they really don't know what they did, or what someone said they did. . . . Carl didn't know what he did, for a good reason. "Lisa Carbottle," Carl sneered. The principal's session dragged to a stop. —But I'm getting ahead of myself, let's go back to recess. . . .

Lisa liked running. At recess today no one was playing the usual games she liked, so she just ran. She liked the feel of the wind in her hair, the ground whizzing by, and the sensation of flying . . . flying? "Wha— whoa, ahhh!" Lisa landed with a thud, and hit her head right on a rock. Lisa caught her breath.

Emilia, the spoiled brat, yelled to the recess aide, "Carl threw a rock at Lisa, and it hit her on the head!" Before he knew it, the big recess aide was hauling him away to the principal's office.

Carl, relieved that the session was over, walked back to class. As he rounded the corner he saw Emilia and Lisa in the hall. "I'm going to blame everything on someone," Lisa said, imitating Emilia.

"But why do you care?" Emilia snapped.

"Cause everybody thinks I blamed him, then everybody finds out that it was an accident and they think I'm a jerk for blaming something when it was an accident!" Lisa said without putting in a period. Lisa turned around and saw Carl. "Carl I did'n—"

He cut her off. "I saw the whole thing."

"Oh."

They walked lazily back to the classroom. "What's home like?" Carl asked.

"My mom and dad always want me to be perfect at everything, and if I'm not perfect, he makes me practice, practice, practice." She paused. "What about you?"

"Well . . ." Carl started. "Let's just put it this way, he hits me when he's happy, he hits me when he's sad, and sometimes, he's just happy to hit me." They thought a moment. Carl burst out, "I know!" like he was Einstein creating the atomic bomb.

"Let's do it!" they both yelled, and rushed back to class. The day dragged on. Finally the bell rang and they both rushed out of the classroom. Carl locked himself into a bathroom stall. The kids rushed out to their buses and the school was silent, well, mostly silent. Carl heard a rolling sound coming closer and closer.

The bathroom door opened and he saw boots walking around. "The janitor," Carl whispered. The stall door flung open. Carl was ready. As soon as the door opened Carl dived under the divider into the next stall. He then slowly crept out of the bathroom.

As soon as Lisa heard the rolling sound go into the other bathroom, she crept out the door. She waited and the door opened. She grew tense. It was Carl. "Janitor," they whispered in unison.

"Let's go in there," Carl suggested. "It's used for storage, no one will go in there." Carl and Lisa walked in and heard a janitor approaching. They dove behind some boxes.

Two janitors walked in. One whispered, "Let's do it tonight."

"Which one?" the other said.

"Pod one," he answered.

They walked out. "That was close," said Lisa. "Let's go up." They climbed the boxes, pushed up a ceiling tile and climbed through.

"Wow, it's big up here," Carl said as they stood up. They were inside a vast chamber above the ceiling. There were pipes all over. They saw some boxes, so Carl walked over and opened one. "Hey, they have lights up here," Carl proudly exclaimed.

Lisa walked over. "They must've been left from the ceiling repairers," Carl explained. Lisa blindly found an outlet and plugged it in. "Wow, they're string lights," Carl said. "Like Christmas lights but with bigger light bulbs." They spent the next hour stringing lights.

Carl thought, *I'm just going to pull up a random floor tile and see what's in the room.* The first one was just the janitor supply office. Then he hit the jackpot. The computer lab. He hopped down. "He he," Carl laughed. He heard something outside of the door. Lickety split he was up and putting the tile back.

He heard the voices saying, "Load 'em up." He waited. *Computer Lab . . . Load 'em up!* He sneaked to Lisa crouched by a box. "Lisa!" he whispered, "Someone is stealing the computers!"

"The janitors." She added, "Why them?"

"They said 'pod one.' Computer pod one."

"Oh."

"To the office!"

They ran-walked to where they thought the office might be. "Up!" Carl said as they lifted the tile up. "Bingo." They jumped down.

Before Carl could breathe, Lisa was on the phone. "Nine one one . . . we have a burglary . . . Crestwood Hill Elementary . . . okay . . . bye." Before Carl could process the information Lisa was up in the ceiling. He jumped up. They carefully set the tile down, if anyone would notice a misplaced ceiling tile it would be Mrs. Brown. In the distance they heard sirens, wailing away. . . .

Matthew Ickstadt
Grade 5
Liberty Ridge Elementary School, Woodbury
Writer-in-Residence: Stephen Peters

You Are Going to Get Wet

Water sticks to your clothing
Water sticks to your skin
Water sticks to the grass
And to the fish's fin

And there is one thing that I know
There is one thing that you get
If you hang around water long enough
You're going to get wet

When I go to the pool
And look at the water there
There's always a dip in the middle
And it may give you a scare

When I go to the lake
I see the bugs on top
They keep skating on the surface
Like they'll never stop
They don't sink to the bottom
They don't sink like a stone
Because there is surface tension
They stay up all alone

Standing in the shower
Lying in the bath
Getting doused by a squirt gun
While doing your math
Running through the sprinkler
Washing your pet
If you hang around water long enough
You're going to get wet

Ms. Ross's Class
Grade 4
Dayton Elementary School, Dayton
Musician-in-residence: Charlie Maguire

The Basketball Rap

You talkin' to da man
I'm 7 foot 5
Best player in the nation
I'm on *NBA Live*

When I'm in the game
The whole court is on fire
I got you beat
And don't think I'm a liar

I get the ball in the post
My center clears the way
Slam it home one more time
I've scored 50 today!

I'm the King of the court
You can't steal my crown
I go jackin' up a three
Swish! I knock it down

I plow you down
Like a big bulldozer
You drive in the lane
But you ain't gettin' no closer

You can't catch
What's too fast to see
But don't feel bad
You've been beat by ME!

Daniel Johnson
Grade 7
Oak Hill Montessori School, Shoreview
Writer-in-residence: Sarah Fox

Rolling to Be a Champion

-Refrain-

Roll, roll, roll, rolling
Roll, roll, roll, rolling
Roll, roll, roll, rolling
Rolling to be a champion!

-Verse-

Get the log rolling under your feet
Keep it steady, don't lose the beat
On the log with a friend
Roll that log again and again
You have to have strength and speed
If you want to stay in the lead
Spin it one way, turn it around
Make the other person fall down

Shoes with cork, shoes with spikes
Roll that log day 'til night
All that practice will do you good
Beat the opponent like you should
Laura Marchand she was small
Her spirit was big and she beat them all
It doesn't take size to be the best
To be a better "birler" than the rest

The grand day has finally come
The big tournament has just begun
They roll the log the crowd goes wild
Every man, woman and child
Bounce the log to and fro
Who's the winner, we soon will know
Splash the water in their eyes
Make them fall and take the prize!

Ms. Wilson's Varsity Choir
Music inspired by Derek Schrecengost and Jeff Dunaisky
Grades 9-12
Cloquet Senior High School, Cloquet
Musician-in-residence: Charlie Maguire

Pink Pencil

A pink pencil is like a kid
that loves to eat strawberry
ice cream. A pink pencil
likes to jump off a
bridge and swim in the
Mississippi River. It doesn't
sink because it has invisible
wings that can fly only
when it is in need. The
pink pencil can save people
when they're in trouble or
if they are in a fight.
Pink pencil is like a hollow
log that likes jokes. It's
favorite animal is a killing
Tyrannosaurus Rex. If pink
pencil gets mad, she grumbles
and yells for freedom for
her to win the fight.
Pink pencil goes to Holdingford
Elementary and is in
6th grade. If pink pencil sees a kid
being bullied or in a fight she zaps
their brain and tells them to be
good and nice from now on. Pink
pencil doesn't use a toilet to go
to the bathroom. She uses a napkin.
Pink pencil is allowed to have a new
power on her birthday. This year she
turns 10, so she gets 10 powers.
She never gets cold or hot, she's
always in a comfortable mood or
style. Pink pencil's favorite music
is rock 'n roll.

Kimberely Gielen
Grade 5
Holdingford Elementary School, Holdingford
Writer-in-residence: John Minczeski

FIVE LANES OF DESTINY

My Town

In my town
The grass is lush and green
And the sky a sapphire blue.
The trees in the yards
Stand tall and proud
Like soldiers guarding a priceless treasure.

In my town
The slow rumble of the cars
As they glide down the avenues
Is a sweet lullaby
Playing for all who need to rest.

The children laugh and play tag
In the jungles they call their back yards
As their parents chat on porches.

In my town
You can't walk a block
Without getting a friendly hello
Or a smile that shines like the sun.

The people are close, like a large family
And they're there for each other
When things go for the worst.
This is my town,
My family,
My home.

Jaylin Stroot
Grade 8
Roseau Secondary School, Roseau
Writer-in-residence: Nora Murphy

Home

Home? My home? I don't know where my home is.

My home is not my ancestors' home. My home is not the Land of Eternal War. My home is not where brothers kill brothers. My home is not where bombs burst and limbs get blown off people or where blood spills across the land. My home is not where people judge each other by their tribes. My home is not where people disgrace people and degrade them because they belong to the untouchables of our land.

Most people think that home is where your family came from or where they were born, but there is also another saying, "Home is where the heart is." So what if my heart is not in my ancestors' home? What if it is not where I was born or lived the first four and a half years of my life? Is there anything wrong with that?

My home is where my brother and me fight and where I scream at my siblings. Where the smell of pasta and French dressing hits you in the face when you open the door. My home is where we cook *sambus* and *mandas* for a whole month every year. Home is where I freeze to death waiting for the school bus.

Now do you really believe that home is defined as your origin, or can it be more?

Fadli Mohamed
Grade 11
Ubah Medical Academy, Minneapolis
Writer-in-residence: Nora Murphy

Boom

You hear a boom
and then a thud.
You go around the corner.
You see a crowd.
You go to see
a man
with a bullet wound.
He's been shot.
Get the paramedics someone yells.

Go to his funeral.
It is very sad.
The coffin sinks six feet under.

And I can't help thinking
how many people
has this person who shot
this man hurt?
Because I know
he wasn't the only one.

Taj Mclean
Grade 4
Webster Magnet School
Writer-in-residence: Julia Klatt Singer

Another Family

That summer was long and muggy.
My grandmother
parading around in a form-fitting *ao dai*
covering everything and leaving
nothing to the imagination.
The eye of a soldier she caught
the hair I touch when I touch mine.
The American, nameless.
His pictures she burned
nothing was left except
a charred 8x10.

You saw my mother once
before you went back home
to start another family
of your own.
My eyes burned holes in
the pictures trying to find a
trace of me.
But all I needed to do was
look in the mirror.

Lyly Nguyen
Grade 9
Columbia Heights High School, Columbia Heights
Writer-in-residence: John Minczeski

Immigration from Every Nation

-Refrain-

Immigration from every nation
We send salutation to all of the world
Immigration from every nation
Every situation, every boy and girl

Statue of Liberty
First land we did see
Now it's five lanes of destiny
To the USA

(Refrain)

El Salvador
Mexico opens the door
Cuba to the Florida shore
Of the USA

(Refrain)

Many "*Comidas*" to you
Enchiladas, nachos, tacos, too
Quesidillas, refried beans
To the USA

Let's have a party today
We invite you to come and stay
We'll have a piñata, and the band will play
In the USA

Ms. Pearce's Class
Grade 4
North Intermediate School, Saint Peter
Musician-in-residence: Charlie Maguire

Madeleine

My name is fancy like a
graceful dancer, dancing to
the sound of a million loons.

My name is a Jamaican waterfall,
falling down, down, down.

My name walks the streets
of Paris looking for nothing
in particular.

My name explores the rain forest
looking for a new species of animal.

My name is beautiful like a
model going down the platform.

My name is Madeleine.

Madeleine Hamerski
Grade 5
St. Anthony Park Elementary School, Saint Paul
Artist-in-residence: Marie Olofsdotter

Where I Come From

I come from my mom's belly.
Sometimes I come from school, my neighborhood on the East Side.
Sometimes I come from the sky.

I come from green grass, from mysteries inside my head,
from my writing and a big candy store.
Sometimes I pop out of trees.

I come from my pretty brown eyes, fried chicken, airplanes
my best friends' heads and all our stories.
Sometimes I come from my examples.

I come from my smiles, my face, from my poems.
I come from playing tag, the candy man and many many ideas.
Sometimes I come from cake.

I come from secrets, the alphabet, and school work
from cotton candy and music. I come from a lot of love.
Sometimes I come from storms.

I come from my crying, and good hot dogs. I come from math,
from writing, from reading, and experiments.
Sometimes I come from spider webs.

I come from planets, from Pa Nhia's head. I come from all
my teachers, from everything they've taught me.
Sometimes I come out and bloom.

Curtesa Scott
Grade 4
Webster Magnet School
Writer-in-residence: Julia Klatt Singer

Life is Priceless

Definition of what life is, priceless. Tell you the definition of price-less, you like it? Good, so why don't I learn to just let it go?

I'm sitting on the floor all alone, on the phone, talking to my daddy that never comes home.

First comes depression, then comes pain, then it hurts so bad that it drives you insane.

As I lie awake in my bed at night, wondering if things will be all right. As my breathing quickens, my air is thickening. My emotions run deep, it gets to the point where I'm too scared to sleep.

Meanwhile daddy out dealing, then he does some stealing. Mama didn't want to put up with it so years ago she said that we were leaving. When I thought she was just teasing.

But as I stand here before you now, I don't show evidence that it's putting me down. Never to let my feelings be seen, I'm playing it clean, for myself, the only member on my team.

Because when nobody else will, I treat myself like a queen, and that's just how my world should be, perfect in every single way just for me.

I've been to Grand Marais all the way to LA, down to Tampa Bay on the FLA coast. I usually don't brag, I mostly boast.

This is my life, my life is my price, can't you tell by the way I work my style and stride?

My life has been a test, no sorry sob story at its best. Just take a look at this marvelous success.

Mykaylah Rowlison
Grade 6
Middleton Elementary School, Woodbury
Writer-in-residence: Tou SaiKo Lee

Half a World Away

I am the tan house
With the blue garage door—a replica of
One half a world away.
I am Rapunzel, the long golden hair
Tumbling, bouncing down the tower.
I am the dark, impenetrable, Banisher of Warmth
I am all books, nearly lost in forests of memory
I am a Laura Ingalls Wilder book, read curled
Up by the fire.
I am dogs barking in the night, disturbing sleep of all
I am skiing, rushing down a mountain, wind whipping,
Howling like a demon.
I am the warm ocean and dirt roads of Ocracoke,
One place not touched by civilization's
Modern messes.
I am that little girl, jumping on the bed at night,
Christmas lights twinkling down,
Colored stars in a dark room.
I am the King Charles spaniel from across the street,
Spinning, a tiny whirlwind, for a treat.
You'll find me there, with the blue garage door, a replica of
One half a world away.
I am that tan house.

Miel Jasper
Grade 7
The Blake Middle School, Hopkins
Writer-in-residence: John Minczeski

Eyes Full of Sky

I have the olive skin
of my father
the one
whom I've never known
Italian heritage
which I've never known

Anna is Hebrew
for Grace

I am not Jewish
but am part
of a culture
I do not understand

the dark eyes
of my 10 aunts and uncles
Ken Kari, possibly David,
Glenn, Keith, Erik and Mark,
Elaine, Mary Jo . . .
Matthew was of
corn silk and
eyes full of sky

Lucia is Italian
and Latin
meaning light
as if I,
a dark-haired,
dark-minded child
was a light
in the darkness.

the infamous
cow lips
the dreaded and prized
lips made for
the unknown

Pax
Latin for peace
describes me
in detail . . . perhaps

an activist

the eyebrows my
aunts and mother
love for some reason
proud of curves
I hate

Knapp
the German trait
of farmers
and shaking heads

Anna Lucia Pax Krupp
Grade 7
The Blake Middle School, Hopkins
Writer-in-residence: John Minczeski

Run Away Hometown

When I was born,
My soul was as hard as a diamond,
As I watch every day pass
I'd laugh, sing and play
I knew I was happy
Until, the day was the day

The wind's arm pulled me to another direction
I left my hometown, not realizing
I also forgot my happiness
Not knowing who to blame
Because things were not the same

Not knowing any faces,
Going to strange places,
"Is this the place I'm going to stay?"
I ask myself
Do I remember the day I was born?
Or was I too little to realize it was gone?

Saray Roeun
Grade 8
Hazel Park Middle School, Saint Paul
Writer-in-residence: Tou SaiKo Lee

The Day at the Races

My voice is as loud as the engine
of the race cars racing down the race track.
My brain cells are like the pit crew
working on the car and putting
new tires on.

My mind is as daring
as Carl Edwards's mind when he does his back flip
off his car.
My heart is as red as Dale Earnhardt Jr.'s car
speeding down the track.

My hands are as strong as Dale Jarad steering
himself out of a crash.
My feet are as active as Jeff Gordon's feet pressing
the gas pedal.

Logan Raygor
Grade 4
Oak Hill Community School, Saint Cloud
Writer-in-residence: Susan Marie Swanson

It's Okay to Cry

It's okay to cry. That is one of the things that was said to me over and over by family, friends, people that knew what was going on, and the people I had just met. I was fourteen at the time that my dad was diagnosed with a disease called ALS. ALS is a disease that eats away the muscles in the carrier's body. Usually the disease takes three to four years to take over a body. In my dad's case it took nine months.

When I first heard that my dad was sick I was devastated, I couldn't keep my thoughts straight, I ran worst-case scenarios through my head over and over until I couldn't think of anything worse. My mother, my father, my sister and I lived in a two-story house with yellow siding and black shingles. We'd been there for seven years and we knew and liked all of our neighbors. My dad had short black hair that he styled a special way every morning, a way that would hide his distinctive balding that he shared with his brothers and father. Computers were his life, he worked with them, he worked on them, in them, and he always had one by his side. From the time I was five till the time my dad got sick, he worked out of town, usually somewhere very far away from Minnesota like California, Seattle, Chicago, or Atlanta.

In late October, early November, the doctor told us that my dad had a maximum of two months to live. He was really weak at that point and there wasn't much he could do. We moved his office up to the living room and we had an automatic chair installed that brought him up and down the stairs. Two times a week a lady from the hospice center came to check up on him. They would give him a lot of things that helped him with his daily life. Hospice is a program that helps terminally ill patients, or people that are dying, cope with their death and try to make them as comfortable as possible.

I couldn't concentrate on anything any more; thoughts were racing around my head at unimaginable speeds. Every day felt like an eternity. The whole situation felt so unreal, it felt like I was constantly in a dream that I couldn't wake up from. School was a great escape for me because when I was there I could put everything behind me and I could actually have something to concentrate on. It's very hard to see someone you love slowly die and not be able to do anything about it.

The last two weeks in December were probably the hardest because the doctor had said a maximum of two months. That could mean anything from a day short of two months, a week, or two weeks short of two months. Every day I was prepared to wake up and hear the news. On Christmas day we stayed home and opened presents. Normally we went over to my uncle's to celebrate with the whole family, but my dad was too weak to go.

On December 29th my dad passed away peacefully and quietly in his sleep. That morning my mom told me what happened. It was so unreal. The sight of a dead person is odd because they look like they're sleeping and you could just poke them and they'd wake up, but that's not the case. My dad was always interested in science so he decided to donate his body to the U of M for scientific research.

That morning I wish I had had a book that told me how to act, how to think, how to feel, and how to break the ice after long periods of silence. But there is no manual for life.

Marty Reichert
Grade 9
Eastview High School, Apple Valley
Writer-in-residence: Laurie Lindeen

Voice

I love the sound of my mother's voice
when she yells at me
because every time she yells at me

it passes through my ears and goes
wherever it wants
as I look at her and think to myself
this lady is crazy.

I love the sound of my mother's voice
when she talks because every word
that comes out
is cleaned out

I love the voice of my mother
when she talks
because every time she speaks
she speaks with her mind wild and open.

Tata McCauley
Grade 10
Patrick Henry High School, Minneapolis
Writer-in-residence: Diego Vázquez

Money Turns to a Drug

Money turns to a drug
Now everyone's fiendin for some
Cause there's not enough going around
So you gotta compete to eat
Or end up six feet deep
A lot of gang bangers constantly walkin the streets
So therefore they must hold heat
And no doubt the streets lurk
So you gotta stay alert
See we all grew up in the streets of St. Paul
And most of us don't care bout the law
And some even turn to outlaws
But we all gotta survive stay alive
No one wants ta see the day y'all life flashes
Back to the day of your birth
So as long as we're here we ain't leaving this earth
Well I ain't leaving at least not without a fight
Through the night under the night light of the streets
Cuz I'm a street fighter
My flows gotten tighter and white tees
Staying brighter than my earring with the ice
Yeah I eat rice staying alive watching hood soldiers
Fall on the battlefield dang their fate and doom has been sealed
Can't you feel the fears of everyday strife
Wakin up every day thinking it could be my life
Yeah I got growin pains and when it rains
I pour a 40 for my friends and families in the ground
Always be missin them around remembering when we used to clown
Those were the days of our lives
When we didn't have to worry about getting stabbed with knives
And getting shot when the block was hot with gangs
And police saying freeze but now we livin a better life where
Memories are in the past and not found
Cause we choose to forget the memories of those
Sad times hard times u understand my rhymes

Tyler Vang
Grade 11
Rondo Community Outreach Library, Saint Paul
Writer-in-residence: Tou SaiKo Lee

My Story

Yo my name is j-dog listen to me roar,
Yo my name is j-dog listen to me soar,

I come from a place that is pretty tight except I'm always getting
into a big fight. When I was 11 I came home one night and I was
told, we're moving to Minnesota where my dad's work is bold! Next
thing I know I'm waving to peers and trying to hold back all my wet
tears.

I got to Minnesota and it seemed all right but I was still a little nervous and held my arm tight. Got to my house round 3 or 4, looked
back and got the nerve to open the door. Went to the fridge and got
a pop, just looked at it and blew off the top!

Went to bed around 8 or 9 and listened to the neighbors drunk on
beer and wine.
Couldn't stand that crap, so went to the window and hit the tap.
Tried to fall asleep and that's what I did.

Looked out the window the very next morning, stayed at my house,
it was pretty boring. Very next day I had school failed my first
assignment it wasn't cool, couldn't tell my parents they would be
mad but that was bad. My parents found out the very next day and
now I'm grounded till the end of May!

From Texas to Woodbury that's my story it's all pretty true and I
made it through.

Jared Lonergan
Grade 6
Lake Junior High School, Woodbury
Writer-in-residence: Tou SaiKo Lee

Dragons

My hair is as black
as the European
dragon's scales.
My blood is as pure
as a dragon's heart.
My eyes are as
sharp as a
dragon's tooth.
My imagination is like
a dragon flying over
clear water
of the Pacific Ocean.
My mind is a dragon
breathing hot
fire through
the sky.

Davis Wodek
Grade 4
Chanhassen Elementary School, Chanhassen
Writer-in-residence: Susan Marie Swanson

The Tree of Magical Cookies

It was windy outside and Riley was walking in the woods like she always did on Friday nights. Riley tripped over a big stick. When she fell, she saw a huge shadow. Riley stood up and saw a large tree with a tiny pink wooden door. When she was close to the door, she could hear loud machines. Riley heard a high-pitched voice saying, "I have finished eight dozen!" When Riley heard that, a question popped up in her mind. *Eight dozen of what?* She was anxious to find out.

Riley opened the little wooden door. When she opened it she saw large ovens and tiny elves! Some of the elves were carrying trays of fresh baked cookies. They smelled like magic. Riley went to an elf and said, "Where am I?"

"The Tree of Magical Cookies," said the elf. "I am the head elf, my name is Che Che." Riley was confused about everything she was seeing.

Che Che took Riley to a big room filled with hundreds of tables, with different cookies on them. "Try one," Che Che said. Riley couldn't resist. She had to try one! So finally after thinking about it she took one. Riley took the star-shaped one with purple sprinkles that smelled like peppermint. She took a big bite and then Riley felt a little weird inside. Che Che said, "You might be able to do things that you could never do before!"

"Will I ever get better?" Riley questioned.

"Only when you discover your power," said Che Che. Riley didn't know what to do.

Che Che led her to a room that she could stay in. Riley lay on the bed. She wondered why no one was friends in the old tree? Riley realized that maybe she didn't have a super power. Maybe she had the power to make all the elves friends again.

Riley went up to an elf that she had never met. The elf said, "Hi," in a different language.

Without even knowing, Riley said, "Hi," back, in the same language. Now Riley knew why all the elves weren't friends. They couldn't speak to each other. Riley now could speak whatever language the elves were speaking. Riley had a plan.

She told each of the elves, "Come to the room full of tables." When Riley was done talking to each elf, she went to the room. Riley told the elves that "All the elves should make up one elf language!" Riley was being the translator for the elves. All the elves were grateful to Riley for her help. Now since this day, all elves have one language and are all friends. Riley doesn't have powers anymore, but since helping the elves, she has never felt better.

Hailey Pietraszewski
Grade 4
Madison Elementary School, Blaine
Writer-in-residence: Stephen Peters

Mental Warp

I'm falling down the stairs
I fall up to the attic
the crows tell many lies
they're stirring up the static
I'm sitting in the darkness
my wall, it has a pulse
it whispers many stories.
I wonder which ones are false
I'm lying in the crawl space
the dead rats are dancing
I hear the old man laughing
and the ground begins cracking
I'm staring out the window.
the wind, it's staring back at me
its screams out many horrors
but the sound, it comes from me.

George Schumacher
Grade 10
Patrick Henry High School, Minneapolis
Writer-in-residence: Diego Vázquez

Karate Wolf

Chapter 1: A Deadly Tradition

It all started the day I finished karate school. I was being chased by two men in black clothing! I knew that if I could make it to my jet I could fly away over the horizon, then I would be safe. My heart was like a racecar engine and my fur was sweating like crazy! BOOM!!!!!!!!!! There were more of them and one had a bazooka! BOOM!!!!!!!!!!!!!!! I was almost there. BOOM!!!!!!!!!!!!!!!!!!!!! It could be risky, but I decided to do a flip into my jet and I just made it! BOOM!!!!!!!!!!!!!!!!!!! I heard as I was flying away. Then I remembered that was a traditional way of sending people, or wolves in this case, off.

Chapter 2: An Unexpected Visitor

I looked up to see my pet lizard gecko staring at me. "I told you to stay at the mansion," I said.
    "I wanted to make sure you made it," he replied.
    Right then we were hit with a missile! I watched as everything went in slow motion. I was falling and that was the last thing I remember before we hit Kawaii Island.

Chapter 3: Island of Doom

When I finally woke up I felt extreme heat. We must have landed near a volcano. I started to move away but I was weak. It would be extremely hard and risky to make it to the forest but I decided to try. It took me four hours to get to the forest and two more hours to find a shelter. It was a nice little cave. I turned on my TV watch and made some coffee. Just then I heard a BOOM! I looked out of the cave and saw Indians with rocket launchers.
    "Wow," I said. "Here, have some coffee," I said, not sure my idea would work. While they were having coffee, I snuck out and ran and I fell into the ocean!

Chapter 4: Pirates of the Caribbean

I swam until I saw a boat in the distance. I swam to the boat as fast as I could. When I reached the boat, I was greeted by grubby-looking men who stunk like outhouses. They tied me up with ropes and said, "You'll be walkin' the plank today, matey!" while they were licking ice cream cones.

The End.

Coming soon: *Karate Wolf 2*

Chapter 1: Island of Life

My name is Turbo. If you've read *Karate Wolf* you know what's happening. If you haven't, I'm in water with my arms and legs tied together.
    Then I suddenly had an idea! I would do the back float till I reached land. So I went with my idea. After all, I had no choice. So I floated for days, then I fell asleep. When I woke up I found myself on a deserted island. It had a cave and a spring and five fruit trees and six plum trees. Then I realized how hungry I was, so I picked some fruit. It tasted better than anything I ever tasted!

Mitchell Zabel
Grade 4
Rice Elementary School, Rice
Writer-in-residence: Lisa Bullard

Unexpected Aliens

It all started on an ordinary day. Or at least it seemed ordinary. Little did I know that some very unordinary things were about to happen. Suddenly, the clouds darkened, the wind got faster and a UFO came flying out of the sky. It came down and landed on my driveway. Thinking fast, I dove behind a tree. Two aliens walked out of the UFO.

"NiveD deman eno eht si erehw?" shouted one of the aliens.

"Su thiw emoc tsumeh!" yelled the other.

I quickly saw that they spoke backward. I translated that to "Where is the one named Devin?" and "He must come with us!"

I thought for a moment. I realized that aliens are probably very easy to trick. Then I had an idea.

"Sunev no revo sevil eh. Esouh gnorw eht evah uoy," I told them.

"Yrros os era ew. Ho," one said.

"Snoitcerid eht rof sknaht tub," said the other alien.

"Emoclew era ouy," I replied.

Then they flew off. I realized that I just saved myself from going with some strange aliens.

Devin Kelly
Grade 4
Chanhassen Elementary School, Chanhassen
Writer-in-residence: Kelly Barnhill

The Dream that Came Alive

One day I fell into a dream and started spinning all around. When I had stopped to twirl and spin, I looked to see what I could see but all it was, was blue.

Then I fell a foot or two. The world came into focus. And there and then I saw the thing I liked best, among the bed of daffodils, the little spot of roses, I saw a large pink mushroom with yellow spots all over it. And when I hit that soft grassy ground I sat right under it, peacefully, just sitting there.

Then a hole opened right under me.

The hole was huge and black. It pulled me, totally, against my will. I tried to scramble out, but it pulled me down down down. I was falling through tunnel after tunnel until I hit the hard rock floor. I felt dizzy. I swayed, but pulled myself up. I stood in the middle of a hall lit by torches which blazed in my eyes as I walked down the hall, thoughts flung in my head about what happened, about wanting to be back in my soft bed, and wondering how I would ever get out.

Suddenly I was jerked out of my thoughts to find a giant ant. A rock, a rock was all I had to defend myself. I threw it straight at the ant's head. In a minute I knew I had made a mistake. About one hundred more ants emerged from the dark. They chased me through the tunnels, their pinchers at my heels. I ran as fast as I could until I saw a round circle of light. I climbed out the hole to find myself in my room. To find myself sitting up in my bed looking straight at a little ant farm on my dresser.

Julia Brooks
Grade 4
Normandale French Immersion School, Edina
Writer-in-residence: Julia Klatt Singer

In the stomach of . . .

The grass was eating me whole
but I got away because a bird
came and ate me,
now I'm sitting in his stomach
wondering what is all this slimy stuff is,
I think it's a worm . . . maybe not.
I'll probably be in here awhile
my hand is touching something,
what is it?
Oh, gosh, it's another human!
We started talking a bit.
He said he's been here in since 1996.
It is now 2007.
I asked him what he eats.
"Whatever comes in."

Katie Hoff
Grade 7
Roseau Secondary School, Roseau
Writer-in-residence: Diego Vázquez

Towering 3

Beth and her friends, Lily and Allie were walking through the woods. Soon at the middle of the woods they saw a clearing, which they'd never been to before. "Weird," Beth said. "I thought we covered every inch of this wood."

"Me too," Allie said, puzzled.

They walked into the clearing. They heard squirrels chattering. Suddenly, from out of nowhere, a tower shot up from under their feet. They were going up, up, up and UP!

As suddenly as it had started, it stopped. They started climbing down. Soon, about five feet below, they crawled into a window. "This is crazy!" Lily screamed.

They had crawled into a little room with one bed and two blankets and pillows on top of it. There was no door. "It seems strange there are three brushes on the bureau," Beth said, puzzled.

"It seems they were waiting for us," Lily said.

"They who?" Allie asked.

Just then a witch burst through the ceiling carrying a loaf of bread as thin as cardboard. "Hey, you're not Rapunzel!" the witch exclaimed. "Oh well, now I have three captives!"

Then a wolf swung through the window. "Where are those pigs?" he yelled.

Then a glass slipper crashed against the wall. "Hah, no you have no proof you were ever even at the ball," a squealing voice said.

"You old hag, uh, I mean, please stop!" A voice you could only assume was Cinderella.

"Stop it everyone!" Allie cried.

"Oh, everyone sit!" Beth ordered. Everyone sat.

"Come up here you two!" Beth commanded. Up they came. Cinderella and Anastasia came up and sat on the yellow comforter. The wolf sat on the bureau. The witch sat on the mending basket.

"Okay, everyone state their case."

"No."

"Don't wanna."

"No thank you."

"Shut up."

"Let me throw them out the window," Lily suggested.

"No, I want them to talk it out," Beth said firmly.

"I want them out of my tower," the witch said under her breath.

"Okay, but how shall we get us out?" Cinderella wondered kindly.

"Beth, she's right." Allie and Lily said in unison.

"Why is she right? She's just a dust maid," Anastasia said.

"Beth, isn't your dad out here this time of day?" Lily asked.

"You have that whistle . . ."Allie started.

"Yeah!" Beth said excitedly.

"It won't work," the witch said. "It's a fairy tale forest."

"Let's have an instant replay backwards," Allie suggested. "Then the tower should shoot down instead of up."

So they started up the tower. They said what they said backwards, "weird is this." Etc., etc., etc. Then the tower shot down.

Then Beth woke up! "Oh, it's just a dream!" she said. That same day she went back to the same place the tower was. Nothing happened. "I guess it was a dream!" But when she talked to Allie and Lily, they remembered the same dream too.

Mysteries . . . never can explain them!

Taylor Kiemele
Grade 4
Park Elementary School, Le Sueur
Writer-in-residence: Stephen Peters

Pegasus

Once upon a time there was a boy who rode on a flying horse named Pegasus. He tried to do tricks on Pegasus, but he failed. Even because of this he still wanted people to watch him. He really wanted to straddle Pegasus. When people came to see him try they just laughed. But some people liked him. But those people could not tell anyone else about him because nobody knew his name. Even he did not know his name.

Once when he was flying another flying horse came and got in a fight with Pegasus! The boy could hardly stay on. The horse bit Pegasus's wings off. Pegasus tumbled to the ground. The boy fell with her. They landed in a forest.

The boy picked up his torch and got on Pegasus. The forest was dense and Pegasus's wings were bitten off. They could not fly out, and the forest was too thick to find your way out. The boy was scared. Pegasus started trotting. Then she slowed down. The forest smelled like dead leaves. They could not tell if it was day or night. An owl screeched and Pegasus jumped. The boy fell and hit his leg on a hard stump. He got up and limped toward Pegasus. They napped on the soft leaves. Then they kept going. They rode through the forest. It was as dark as a bear's fur.

Then they came to a cabin. They went in. They saw a piano. The boy tried to play it. It sounded like a screech owl. Suddenly they heard a gust of air. They were scared. They ran into the cellar. The boy had never been in a cellar. It smelled like a pond covered with algae.

He ran back up the stairs and bumped into Pegasus. They both ran out of the cabin. The boy got on Pegasus. They rode into the gloomy forest.

Suddenly he heard a voice calling, "Perseus! Perseus!"

The boy was scared. The voice sounded like a ghost. "Who is Perseus?" he asked.

"You," said the voice.

Pegasus was happy. He trotted toward the voice. A man stepped from the bushes. He said he would heal Pegasus's wings.

"Thank you," said Perseus.

The man taught Perseus how to straddle Pegasus. Everyone liked him and everyone knew his name. He got to be in the Olympics. He won the flying horse race. He was famous and Pegasus was very happy.

But Perseus wondered who the man was. He had never seen his head. He never knew.

Amelia Broman
Grade 2
Oak Hill Elementary School, Saint Cloud
Writer-in-residence: Stephen Peters

Questions of Thinking

Is there one Satan or one in all of us?
Is heaven paradise?
Is Hell Satan's dome or God's prison?
Who takes the bite out of the moon?
Do door handles shake hands with those who open them?
Do 2x4s remember the view they used to have?
Is it always light in heaven or are there dark spots?
Do we form nightmares or do nightmares take
our deepest secrets and form themselves?
Is the moon a boy or a girl?
Are bullets souls stained with the blood
of the innocent?
Are our tears demons leaving us?
When is the end of tomorrow?
Does good have a shaded half?

Paige Weldon
Grade 7
LeSueur-Henderson Middle School, Le Sueur
Writer-in-residence: Dana Jensen

The Saddle Mystery

I listened to the sound of the children talking loudly, excited about the ending of another long school day. I, too, was excited to get home to my rural farm and go riding on my horse, Penny. Penny's hair was as bright as a copper penny. "Katie, want to go riding when we get home?" my 12-year-old sister, Ally, asked eagerly.

"Sure!" I replied happily. Unlike some other sisters, Ally and I like to hang out together. The bus pulled up at our farm. Ally and I stepped out of the bus. We raced into the kitchen, grabbed a chocolate chip cookie and ran into the barn. The barn smelled of hay and manure. My sister and I ate the delicious chocolate chip cookies. We went over to the horse's stable. I went over to where I keep Penny's saddle. It wasn't there!

I raced around Penny's stable trying to find the saddle. At that moment, Ally came in. She asked worriedly, "Have you seen my saddle?"

"No!" I replied. We raced into everybody else's stable in our barn. We found everything in its place except our saddles. I pushed aside the hay. It was as rough as sandpaper.

"Come on, let's tell Mom!" Ally cried nervously. We ran into the house. On the way, my cowboy hat fell off. We rushed into our porch. It was covered by a screen. It was a great place to read on rainy days. But the porch was the last thing on my mind.

"Mom!" I shouted the second I came into the house.

"Have you seen the saddles?" Ally asked my mom.

"Are they where we usually put them?" she asked calmly. My mom was always as calm as an owl when things happened.

"No!" we replied at the same time.

A look of fear flashed across my mom's face.

"What?" I asked worriedly

"Well, yesterday there was a robbery at the Wilson's. They got away with the saddles."

A thought crossed my mind. I ran into our little sister Lizzie's room. She loves detective stuff and has tons of detective kits. One of them has fingerprint stuff that can tell the fingerprints that have been there. I burst into Lizzie's room. It looked like her room should be a rock star's room. I explained to Lizzie what had happened.

She said, "Sure! You can use it!"

I hurried out into the barn with my sisters right behind me. "I am about to figure this out!" I declared.

I hustled over to the barn door's handle. I sprinkled some of the powder onto the door. Fresh fingerprints came into view.

"I've seen those prints before!" declared Lizzie.

"So have I," I added. "Wait a minute! Those are Bobby Aler's fingerprints! I saw them on our glass window!"

We ran into our attics where we keep our extra saddles. We each grabbed one. We raced into the barn. We threw the saddles on the horses so fast it was like they were hot. We galloped to Bobby's house. When we got halfway there, I said, "You guys wait here!"

I snuck into the barn. Sure enough, all our saddles and more were in his barn. I grabbed as many as I could. I loaded them on to Penny. The saddles were all different colors of brown. At that moment, Bobby came in.

At first he looked alarmed, but then he looked mad. "Hey, you're not supposed to be in here!"

I jumped onto Penny and galloped away. Bobby jumped on to Thunderbolt, his horse. As I rode by Ally and Lizzie, I yelled, "Come on! He's following us!" At that moment, I had an idea. "Follow me!" I yelled over the hoof beats. The sound sounded like a herd of elephants. I raced off towards the police station with Ally and Lizzie right behind me. Right behind them was Bobby.

As I reached the little police department, I stopped. "Bill!" I yelled. Bill was an old friend of my mom's. He was a police officer. Bill came rushing out as if the building was on fire. I explained to him what was happening just as Ally and Lizzie were pulling up behind us.

At that moment, Bobby pulled up. He almost ran over Bill.

"Young man, I believe that you'll have to come in and talk to me." Bobby went in and Bill followed. Right before he went in he said, "Girls, thanks for catching him for me!"

Just then, Mom pulled up. "Hi mom!" Lizzie said happily. "Guess what we did today?"

While Lizzie and Ally explained what happened, I thought of Bobby. I felt sort of bad for him. "Come on, girls!" Mom said. "Let's go home."

A few weeks later, I was scanning the paper when I came across an article that said, "Saddle Thief Caught at Last." I read the article. Bobby was forced to give back all the saddles and pay a fee. I was so happy because Bobby was caught and did not have to be sent to juvie. I was so glad that everything turned out all right.

Meghan Kuemmel
Grade 4
Grey Cloud Elementary School, Cottage Grove
Writer-in-residence: Stephen Peters

My New Power

Chapter 1: My New Discovery

My name is Claire. I am 16 years old. I just found out something very weird about a couple days ago. I have a power! I can turn myself invisible! How I found this out was I was walking to my friend, Kayla's house, then this man came.

He didn't look too friendly! In fact he had a big scowl on his face. I was afraid, I was afraid that he would take me somewhere that nobody would find me and that I would not be able to get out of. Before I knew it he was charging at me so I hid behind a bush. He noticed so he went there too.

But when he got there he didn't see anything! He got there right away and I'm not that quick. I looked at my hands because they felt kind of weird and guess what I saw? Nothing!

Completely nothing! Finally he went away.

"Phew, that was close," I said, and went to Kayla's house, still invisible. When I got there we played a few games and studied together for our history test.

Chapter 2: The Pixies

After I was done studying, I went home. While I was driving home, I was thinking of whether I should tell my parents or not. Then these two little pixies showed up on my shoulders. One looked like a devil and one looked like an angel.

"Who are you and what are you here for?" I asked.

"What do you think we are here for, haven't you seen the movies?" the devil said.

"Don't mind him," the angel said.

"Don't mind him," the devil mimicked.

"We are here because we are going to tell you if you should tell your parents or not! Gosh!" the devil said.

"But before we do let's tell you our names," the angel said. "My name is Keisha."

"And my name is Horns," said the devil.

"Now I think you *should* tell your parents, besides you should always tell your parents what is going on in your life," said Keisha.

"Well of course I say the opposite, I think you should *not* tell your parents, besides, don't you want to play some tricks on anybody?"

said Horns.

"Well, I do want to play a trick on my brother, Cole," I said. "I won't tell my parents but I will play a few tricks on my sister," I said.

"Darn it, everybody *always* takes his side, I quit!" Keisha threw her halo on the floor. Then Horns did the Cha-cha.

Chapter 3: The Big Plan

I thought of a great idea! My brother really likes to double-dutch, so when he comes out at recess (we are twins so we are in the same grade so then I won't get in trouble), I will come out, spin the ropes around him a lot, then I will pull it and then that will make him spin into the Girls' Bathroom! It's brilliant!

Chapter 4: The Big Trick

There he is! Oh, I can't wait to pull this off! So I spun the rope around Cole, then pulled it, then he went in the Girls' Bathroom! But then, when he came out he did something he never did before. He started crying!

I felt really bad.

I came up to him and apologized to him. I also told him my secret and what's been happening since I found out about my secret. He took it pretty well. I don't know if he believed me, but it didn't really matter.

Chapter 5: Telling My Parents

I was glad that was over with, but I still had something on my mind. *Oh yeah*! Now I remembered. I had to tell my parents.

I went home and in my most politest and sweet voice, I said: "Mom, Dad, I have something to tell you and it's very important."

"What is it, honey?"

"I've been through a lot of crazy things," I began, "and I haven't told you, so I'm going to tell you. I-I-I have a power to turn myself invisible."

"Hahahahahahahhahaha. Oh, that's a good one, Claire," they said, laughing hysterically.

"No, I'm telling the truth. I promise. I'll show you."

I turned myself invisible and my parents just stood there, with their mouths wide open. "I-I-I don't know what to say," Dad said.

"That's amazing! How did you do it?"

"I don't know, I just did it," I said.

"Well, okay, I guess we have to believe you."

Keisha showed up on my shoulder and whispered in my ear: "You've done good kid, you've done good."

Chapter 6: The End

Well, that's the end to my story. My parents believed me, my brother forgave me, and everything turned out great!

Lauren Poepping
Grade 4
Rice Elementary School, Rice
Writer-in-residence: Lisa Bullard

Special Secret Poem

I hide my secret inside
elephant's ears
in the footsteps of a giant
in the dot of the letter "i."
I hear my secret from
the tick-tock in the clock
from my secret to
my heart
to the east, west, north and south.
Secrets live in
the apple of your eye.

Ellie Wolfe
Grade 2
St. Joseph's School, West Saint Paul
Writer-in-residence: Dana Jensen

The Bronze

I sat in the room looking out the window on an ordinary day in Ms. Gilbertson's room, when suddenly the door creeped open, making a *keri, keri* sound. I looked back, frightened and shocked in the heart but brave in the eyes and outside.

The creature, or human being, or whatever, was standing outside the door. His shallow eyes faced the ground as his hood covered half of his face. He was wearing a black robe that covered his legs completely. He had a white beard that was long all the way to his chest. His fingers were long, but not too long. On his right hand, he held the tiniest marble ever. It was shiny. It was bronze. It was *the* bronze. The Bronze. Behind him was all dark and smoky.

"Are you the one who could help?" he asked.

"Help with what?" I replied.

"My family."

"Who's asking?"

He walked in, taking slow, easy, careful, extraordinarily perfect steps. I looked with wonder.

"This," he said. He brought his right hand out and opened it slowly. "This is the missing puzzle piece. If we stuck it in, the gate shall open and we'll make it safely. But, there are dangers ahead in the way to the gate." He looked at me. "Are you fit and ready?"

"Of course," I said. "When do we go?"

"As soon as we're ready," he answered.

"Um, no offense, but aren't you going to dress up like a real human being?" I asked.

"I am smart enough to know that!" he snapped back.

After ten minutes I started to introduce myself. I mean, we can't be partners working together and we don't know each other. "Well, hello. My name is Sylvia," I said.

He looked at me as if I was lying and he said, "What?"

"Sylvia."

"Well, my name is Black Pearl. B.P. for short."

"Is that your real name?" I asked.

"It is how I am known."

The introduction went on and we decided that we should start out tomorrow.

Endurance Ehimen
Grade 7
Hazel Park Middle School, Saint Paul
Writer-in-residence: Kelly Barnhill

Biggest Umbrella

I have the biggest umbrella.
It picks me up into the sky
with huge blows of wind.
Black outside, rainbow inside
with stars and moons
along the handle.
I take it outside on sunny days
to hide my skin from the light.
I take it out in the rain
just so I have something
to dance with.
Twirling and splashing
in the puddles,
I don't care if I get dirty,
or sopping wet.
Because I have the biggest umbrella.

Chole Poole
Grade 10
Patrick Henry high School, Minneapolis
Writer-in-residence: Diego Vázquez

The Ice Cream Code

"Ugh. You beat me again," said Carl, sitting on the couch.

"Na na na. I beat you, I beat you," said Carl's little brother, Anthony.

"You're just turning ten and I'm twelve and you still act like a little jerk," yelled Carl. Carl dropped the joystick and said, "You stupid, immature baby."

"Kids, it's time to eat," their mom yelled.

"Just a sec, I'm beating Carl's high record," Anthony said in a sarcastic voice, a voice that made Carl want to throw up.

"Mom, Anthony is messing with me."

"No dessert if you keep fighting."

"Mom, what's for dessert?"

"Ice cream."

Carl thought to himself. That is his favorite, and nobody knows about the code.

"Carl hurry up, your food is getting cold and your brother is halfway done," mom yelled loudly. Carl didn't realize that at least five minutes had passed.

"Okay, Mom." Carl rushed downstairs out of his room that he shared with his brother, to the kitchen, and sat down at the end of the table. Anthony was done and got the video game in the room to finish his game of Mortal Combat: Deadly Alliance. Carl's mom was also done cooking and had left when Carl sat down to go to a Saturday afternoon meeting. Carl was done with his cornbread and was eating chicken when his cell phone started ringing.

"We need you now, Agent Black. Someone has stolen the info we have on the code," said a voice that was known to Carl as Park Hazel. Carl was happy to hear that voice. "Agent Black, we know the robber was living in a smelly, cracked up apartment. One more thing, you must be relocated to a house in the hills and it smells like heaven and is beautiful and has a very nice carpet. Get on the job, and the relocation will happen in a month."

"Okay, I'm coming to the agency to get me some gear."

Carl hung up the phone and rushed out of the door. His friend, James Hagg, yelled from across the street, asking to play baseball. Carl yelled back saying he couldn't play.

Carl was still running and had looked back to see where James was and fell blindly over an unfamiliar rock. He got up as fast as he could and ran. He noticed a guy in all black staring at Carl from the left across the street. The passage wasn't that far now. When Carl reached the passage, he took a quick look all around and saw some guy. When Carl was opening the door, he saw that same guy running towards him. The guy running towards Carl jumped up.

"Who are you and what do you want?"

"I am a secret agent from the FBI undercover," said the man in black.

"But that means you're from my agent. Why are you tracking me down?"

"You are in a place where you shouldn't be. They have set explosives on the door. Follow me," the man in black said. The guy in black walked off with Carl. "You were followed to your base," the agent said until he was interrupted by Carl's cell phone ringing.

"Hello," Carl said into the phone.

"The guy you were talking to is a double agent. Break free and come to the base for more info."

"Okay," Carl said angrily.

"Who was that?" the guy in black said.

"Ugh . . . it was my mom. She doesn't know I'm a secret agent. I have to go clean my room."

Carl hung up the phone and tried to run, but the other agent pulled out a gun and held it to Carl's head and said, "Your days are numbered unless you tell me the code."

James Stuckey
Grade 7
Hazel Park Middle School, Saint Paul
Wrier-in-residence: Kelly Barnhill

Pencil's Life Cycle

My pencil is like a scholar.
It is a magical place where words are waiting
in the lead to be chosen. Words are
sad to leave their home. They are happy
to be on a memory paper.
When the words get read, they try
to look their best. When words get
erased, they start as a baby again.
My pencil writes and writes its way
to its destiny.

Abby O'Callaghan
Grade 2
Glen Lake Elementary School, Hopkins
Writer-in-residence: Susan Marie Swanson

The Elf of Terabal

Prelude to the Gage and Christos series

Chapter 1

Every night the same thoughts went through Fexyan's head. He found nothing different about himself. He was tall, elegant and agile, like any other elf would be. The light silk sown cover lay on the ground next to him. The sun's rays crept through the branches, blinding Fexyan. He rolled over, seeing furry paws. The paws of his cat, Norca. Norca puffed up at the sudden movement from Fexyan. She pounced behind a tree fern, then peeked out the side. Noticing it was Fexyan she pranced back, brushing her tail against his face.

After several strokes on Norca's back, she pounced back to her hiding place. Fexyan's father, Vallon, had come in.
Fexyan jerked himself up, grabbing his kilt, belt, vest and over-sash. "Yeah?"

"I was checking if you were awake," Vallon explained, as Norca peered from her spot. "Finish getting dressed, then go the Curer."

Vallon stammered over Norca, who was mewing at his feet.

"Norca, there are plenty of mice in the storage," Fexyan told her, not for the first time.

Vallon had left already, Fexyan guessed; into the thicker part of the woods again.

Fexyan finished by putting Norca in her bed, for she was peering into Fexyan's clothing. Norca was still yet a kitten, and would take any chance she could to rip some cloth to shreds.

It happened before, to his mother, who had two pairs of clothing left from six. She found that mending them would be impossible. Yet, in making new ones, she had no trouble.

Fexyan stepped out of the den. As he had guessed, his father had gone out of the hamlet. The grass was green and lush. Trees were waving upward.

Wait . . . upward? Thought Fexyan

Some wind was coming from the ground. The only explanation was . . . Magic!

Fexyan loved magic! Though he was born a hunter, in the service of catching prey for the Clan, he still found some time in the day to learn the traditional elven sorcery. He rushed toward the source, which was Salvian, a young boy like Fexyan, who was near to becoming forty-four lunares old. Lunares are the elven measurement of time, a different sort of time than which Men call years, but measured by the moon's cycle. A complete cycle of the moon is a lunare. This had changed several times, but finally settled how it was.

The boy, Salvian, was Fexyan's only friend. They had grown up together. Salvian was born a Magus, in the service of sorcery for the Clan. He was the cause of the unnatural winds. Fexyan yelled for Salvian, but he couldn't hear the words come out of his mouth for the winds had grown stronger. Moments later, Fexyan was forced off the ground. Several leaves were pulled from their twigs and Salvian waved his arms shouting what was silence against the wind's roar. The winds slowly weakened, Fexyan fell to the ground, leaves coming after him.

"Err . . ." Groaned Fexyan, grabbing a nearby branch.

"Sorry," explained Salvian.

"Now I have another reason to go to the Curer." Fexyan pulled himself up.

"I have to get back to class," Salvian said, running into the large willow where the sorcery classes were held within a small hold in the center. Fexyan did not have a chance to say goodbye. He still needed to go to the Curer. He sprinted toward the smallest den; the strong scent had already hit him. The mixture of herbs, saps and juices gave it a unique scent, not easily mistaken. Inside, the leaves on the trees were glazed with water dazzling in the morning light. A young lady who was the Clan's Curer appeared from the other side of the den and asked Fexyan kindly to take a seat. They sat on two moss-covered rocks.

"Fexyan, there is something your parents have been wanting to tell you for a very long while now," started the Curer, pushing away leaves and herbs on the large rock between them. "Neither of your parents was born in the Clan, which others have been using to slander you."

Fexyan was now about to run to his den and cry, but he held it in, though feeling a tear trickle down his cheek. Why hadn't they told him? Why were people using that against him? "W-why didn't they tell me?" Fexyan choked out

"Neither of your parents nor I know why."

"What's wrong with them being born out of the Clan?" Two tears were now following the path that the first one had made.

"It's some lie made a long time ago about elves who were not born in the Clan do nothing but bad."

Fexyan could not hold it any longer. He dashed out of the den toward the North Plains, where he knew he would be alone.

"Wait, Fexyan!" called the Curer after him.

It was too late.

To be continued . . .

Chris Murphy

Grade 4

Gordon Bailey Elementary School, Woodbury

Writer-in-residence: Stephen Peters

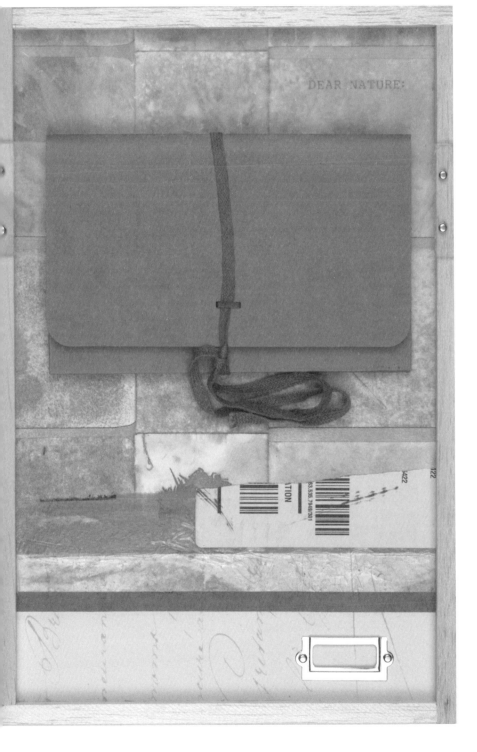

DEAR NATURE:

The Importance of Our Pine Tree

The tree.
That's how we know it.
What we call it.
And when you look at it,
you might think,
it's just a pine tree.
But to me and Sydney,
it's a lot more.
More than a tree.
But a place.
A place where we played.
From being twins
chased by a witch,
to being pixies,
with wings.
Living in a tree mansion.
The tree was a place,
where our imagination
ran free.
A happy place.
Where we could
do anything,
be anything,
have anything.
Our special spot.
We know it as the tree,
And it will always be
Our tree.

Kellie Metzger
Grade 6
Falcon Ridge Middle School, Apple Valley
Writer-in-residence: Diego Vázquez

Dear Swamp

Dear Swamp,
When the spring comes
I catch frogs in you!
And fish. And I camp
by you. I love the way
your waves, lily pads, and
reeds swing and ripple
in the sun. Do you mind
if me and my family call
you Clam Lake, even
though you're a swamp?
At night I hear the
frogs croak, and you smell
as sweet as the birds and
the oak trees and cedars.
It's just so nice. I wish
I lived on you because
I love all your features.

Your Friend,
Jamie Herridge

Jamie Herridge
Grade 2
Mendota Elementary School, Mendota Heights
Writer-in-residence: Susan Marie Swanson

I Am the Shadow

I am the shadow that
haunts you every day. I am
the dark person on the wall.
I am the person that follows
you and copies every move
you make. I am the creature
that never seems to leave.
I am the nightmare in your
dreams. I am the creature
that sits by you every night
breathing in the cool moon
air. I am the person in every
room in every house every
where.

Justin Brown
Grade 4
Meadowbrook Elementary School, Hopkins
Writer-in-residence: John Minczeski

Dear Woods

Dear Woods,
I love to play in you.
You make me feel safe. Do
you remember when my
cousins Jennie and Riley
came over and we built
a fort in you? I can see
birds flying over my head.
I can hear the leaves
crunching beneath my feet.
Sometimes I think that
you are a big castle
and I'm a princess. I like
watching the lake beside
you. I hope you always
remember me. I like to
feel the bark on your trees.
Thank you for growing
there. I wish I could play
in you every day. I like
to play in the mud when
it stops raining on you.
I really hope you remember
me.

Your Second Grade Friend,
Sage

Sage Gegelman
Grade 2
Mendota Elementary School, Mendota Heights
Writer-in-residence: Susan Marie Swanson

River

♪ River, River

Green and yellow walleye swimming by
Orange sun, in the sky
"Old man River" lazy and slow
Don't you wonder where it goes?

River, River, River, River

Blue and purple dragonfly
Lots of them, my, oh my!
"Mighty Mississippi" strong and wide
Turtles on a log, taking a ride

Hummingbirds make a buzzing sound
On the riverbank going around
The kingfisher is the best fisher of all
Crayfish on the bottom they crawl

The mighty bald eagle flies very high
Twenty-five hundred miles of river sky
The catfish burbles are very long
He moves his whiskers to the river song!

Ms. Dawson and Mrs. Geyer's Class
Grade 2
Lindbergh Elementary School, Little Falls
Musician-in-residence: Charlie Maguire

I want to be swept

I want to be swept away
    by life guidance,
the wind that overflows the trees
each morning
    I want to be swept by family support
the water I drink,
    the air that I breathe
I want to be swept into the goodness of my senses.

Chavez Fleming
Grade 8
Hazel Park Middle School, Saint Paul
Writer-in-residence: Diego Vázquez

Dear Cloud

Dear Cloud,
I like it when you make a shape out
of yourself. I remember when I was
on my first airplane and I saw you. You
made me feel all right. If I fall off
the airplane, you would catch me.
Sometimes when I dream about you
I feel like I'm sleeping on you. Cloud,
are you made out of marshmallows?
Sometimes when I'm homesick you make
me feel like I'm at home.

Madeline Hudalla
Grade 2
Mendota Elementary School, Mendota Heights
Writer-in-residence: Susan Marie Swanson

The Trees

And the trees are shaking
in the wind
where I live,
it sounds like
it is music,
I listen every time.
It makes me feel
that I am the wind
making the music
for the people who I love.

Jerry Lee Xiong
Grade 3
Valley View Elementary School, Columbia Heights
Writer-in-residence: Diego Vázquez

The Swan Who Followed Samantha

I'm a swan. I'm
SO! white. Samantha
feeds me bread crumbs.
I follow her all over
the willow tree. I can
fly up to the top
of the tree. I like
her. I follow her into
the tent in the
back yard. I love
her. She loves me.

Samantha Abbott
Grade 1
Aquila Primary Center, Saint Louis Park
Writer-in-residence: Susan Marie Swanson

Fossils

Dinosaur bones and leaves
Shells, footprints and teeth
Fossils are underground
Waiting to be found
Digging deep, deep down
You can find them all around
Fossils are underground
Waiting to be found
Dinosaurs lay their eggs
So, their babies can grow legs
Fossils are underground
Waiting to be found
The eggs are dark, dark, green
In a museum they can be seen
Fossils are underground
Waiting to be found

The soft parts rot away
The hard parts left to stay
Fossils are underground
Waiting to be found

Hard parts covered in sand
Down below the land
Fossils are underground
Waiting to be found

Fossils are really old
Millions of years ago
Fossils are underground
Waiting to be found

Ms. Schabel's Class
Grade 3
Riverview Specialty School, Brooklyn Park
Musician-in-residence: Charlie Maguire

The Dream

"Great," Joey thought. Another *brilliant* idea. While he was hunting in Montana, his older cousin Henry thought they would be able to beat the Parsons in the annual Maple Springs Open Season Hunt-off if they all split up. But as his gullible uncles marched off into the woods that were so thick they were like Jif creamy peanut butter, he felt like he had just landed on the moon and was all alone. Deserted was the first word that came to his mind, event though he knew it wasn't true—but he still felt it. He had been in the mountains for hours since they split up to hunt. He was sure the hunt was over now.

It was getting real dark. The sun was going down as fast at the spring slush dissolves in the coming summer sun. He looked down at his watch blinking 8:37. He would give anything to be back in his trailer park with his mom watching the nightly news.

Pop! The thought came to him as fast as 7th grade football star Jerry Smith could run his famous quarterback sneak. If he got to the top of this mountain, he would be able to see the town and know which way to go. He felt so stupid—why didn't he think of it earlier? He ran up to get the last bit of light, and when he reached the peak, he saw a group of blinking lights in the distance.

He then noticed he had been standing on a cliff.

He thought about the matches his uncle had with him, and that he would do anything to have them right now. His uncles and cousins thought if they got stranded, they would be stranded together, so they carried all the safety equipment.

Joey was starving. He could have eaten six Big Macs. He was trying to think happy thoughts to keep from crying.

Actually, it wasn't that bad. His father was going in and out of rehab hospitals. His mother was taking night college and worked all day. She tried to understand Joey as much as she could, but never did. He was the quiet boy that never talked. This was a good time to be alone.

He picked a spot to bundle up and fall asleep. He pretended to be sleeping in his own lumpy bed, or in his best friend Tony's floor at a sleepover. Tony was his only friend beside Angela, his crush, who he had known since pre-K.

His stomach growled so loud and so long he thought he could use it for a homing device.

The next day, he thought he might be able to shoot something with his .22. Then, he felt his clothes clinging to his body.

"@#*%*!!!!!" He said out loud to himself. His gun was jammed with rainwater in the middle of summer! This couldn't get any worse. He was always the unlucky kid.

Now he would do anything to be with civilization. He was tired of wilderness. He was thirsty, he was cold and hungry. Why was this happening?

He didn't do anything to deserve this. His cousin Henry, out of all people, should have got his. He was the biggest bully anyone could imagine. When the Girl Scout troop came down, he scared all the girls away. He was as ugly as a two-face troll. He could roll his eyes into his head and pull his eyelids up and be a mutant.

He had to find something to drink or he'd die. He looked for puddles to drink from. He faintly heard a rushing water sound to the left. He ran directly toward the sound. It was a small stream and running water! He drank so much and swam in it with his mouth opened and gulping down every drop, including bugs and other creatures. He was so happy; he splashed and drank so much he finally lugged himself out of the water. He felt like a sumo wrestler in a fire suit like the firefighters wore when Mrs. Chan's trailer caught fire. He was sick in the bushes.

He was miserable all day because he couldn't catch food. He was as hungry as a grizzly. He just couldn't find anything. When he went to bed that night, he was cold and delirious. He had a dream.

He dreamed he was flying over a meadow with golden grass. In the middle of the field was his grandpa who was now six months dead. He was in white robes. The only one who Joey could talk to was his grandpa. He and his grandpa had a lot in common. They were always together. They had picnics and went fishing and had had long days together in the arcade. His grandpa said, smiling, "Go to the peak of the mountain and look opposite the town and you will see what you need to see." Then his grandpa flew away.

Joey woke up sweating and hungry (as usual). He looked up at the mountain and saw the peak, and without knowing, got to his feet and started climbing. His arms and legs were screaming to him to stop, but he kept going.

When he finally reached the summit, he turned his back to the town and saw the search party.

Ruby Joy Kinney
Grade 5
Meadowbrook Elementary School, Hopkins
Writer-in-residence: Stephen Peters

A Night to Remember

Walking home
late at night,
everything is quiet
with only the light of the moon
to guide my way.

I stop in the middle of the street
and see a small bird hurt, laying defenseless.
I kneel down
to spot a broken wing.

Afraid to touch the small bird
I step back
get up,
and start walking away.

Lucas Gansmoe
Grade 7
Falcon Ridge Middle School, Apple Valley
Writer-in-residence: Diego Vázquez

Falling

I said,
the sun fell
on my feet
burning my toes.

mom said,
fall asleep
the moon is coming.

Isaac Johnson
Grade 3
Glen Lake Elementary School, Hopkins
Writer-in-residence: Diego Vázquez

.

Talent Show

Claps: that was the audience clapping
loudly for the act before mine.
Ahhhhh! was the voice in my head.
I walked through the open curtain.
Now all I could see were
the flashing lights; they blinded me.
Suddenly the music started,
and, just as fast,
I went into a world of my own.
I could still see the flashing lights
and hear people yelling,
but the screaming in my head was gone.
I felt like there was nothing
to be worried about.
In a flash, it was over
and the clapping was almost as loud
as the grin on my face was wide.

Michelle Atwood
Grade 5
Katherine Curren Elementary School, Hopkins
Writer-in-residence: Joyce Sidman

Life Goes On

Bewildered, I slumped down on my living room couch. My little sister, a little girl of six, had just passed away of a rare heart condition which had caused her to have a heart attack. I couldn't believe it, and neither could my mom, who was sitting opposite from me on the ground, with her eyes closed and her lips fixed in a frown. Finally, unable to restrain myself, I fell into my mother's arms, sobbing my eyes out, deeply saddened that she had to be gone so early on in her life, taking so many memories with her. After just six years here on this Earth, she had been taken away in the blink of an eye.

Around five hours earlier, Jadia and I were playing joyfully on the swing set at nearby Lincoln Park and having a good time when suddenly her face turned as pale as egg whites and her body turned as rigid as a board. Then she collapsed, still as rigid as a board.

Horrified, I screamed, "Help! Help! Something's wrong with Jadia!"

Alarmed, one of our very friendly neighbors, Ernesto Roberts, came running with a serious look on his face because I was soft-spoken and hardly ever screamed. He asked, "What's the matter?"

I tearfully replied, "Jadia and I were playing on the swing set when she turned all rigid and pale. Then she collapsed. I called for help straight away and, luckily, you got here."

He still looked sad, but a quiver of shock ran over his face. Then he quickly said, "Call 911." And, "Wait here."

After what seemed like forever, red and blue lights were flashing everywhere, and a siren blared in my ears. The paramedic that came to get Jadia asked, "Is she your sister?" I nodded though my sobs and gave him my phone number. After the ambulance left, I turned around and headed home.

The phone rang. My mother, still sitting opposite from me, hadn't moved or opened her eyes, and I don't think she breathed, so I just got up, and before grabbing the phone, trembled from head to toe, knowing that this phone call could completely change my life forever.

I put the phone to my ear, and a gruff voice asked, "Is this Jadia Smith's family?"

I answered, "Yes."

He sounded grave as he said, "Well, you should know that your little sister died after three emergency heart surgeries. I'm sorry. But kid, let me tell you something. Don't act like this is the end of the world, kid, because it isn't. Life goes on, kid."

Life goes on. He hung up. The last thing I remember was falling to the floor in a cold faint.

When I regained consciousness, I immediately started to sob. Apparently, my mother had read my actions, because she was still frozen in place and now as white as chalk. No one spoke for ten minutes. Then my mother finally broke the silence by saying, "It's about time that I told you the truth behind Jadia's life. She was diagnosed with leukemia when she was two. Cancer cells were building up in her bloodstream. Unfortunately, we found the tumor too late. Her death was expected. I just wanted her to have the best life she could, until . . ." She broke down entirely, sobbing her heart out. Through the tears, she was saying ". . . I . . . just don't know . . what . . I'll do. . . without . . her . . . "

Three days after that fateful day, the funeral services began. With tears in my eyes, I walked into the dark cemetery. We walked toward Jadia's grave, where her coffin was lying wide open with her lying inside. When we finally got there, I saw her inside the coffin, with the same comfortable and joyful smile on her face, the same smile that she had worn at Lincoln Park. It was all really eerie. I gripped my mother's hand tighter until we were past. We stayed for the funeral services, then silently got in our car, and went home.

At home, everything seemed quiet, creepy, and deathly without Jadia crying or her shrieks of joy to occupy the silent air. In my horribly confused mind, one thought stood out above all the others. *This isn't my home.* I silently went upstairs, and tossing and turning, went to sleep.

Even here, 35 years later, at my new house in San Diego, where I live with my wife and two kids, it all seems like all a big dream, a horrible nightmare.

Sometimes I can still make out noises from Jadia in my deep sanctuary of sleep. But now, one thing has always been planted in my mind. The paramedic's words on that fateful day, "Life goes on, kid. Life goes on."

Do-Hyoung Park
Grade 4
Interdistrict Downtown School, Minneapolis
Writer-in-residence: Julia Klatt Singer

No More Throwing

I think you're done. Sweat, dirt, heat and noise. My dad is giving me the sign for a cutter, telling me how to throw it right. My teammate is pitching right next to me and his dad is listening to him tell what pitches he's going to throw. There are two pitching mounds with big holes made over time from use, sixty feet away are two plates that are scratched up. I am fourteen years old. I am practicing my pitching for the up-and-coming fall baseball season. Follow through and bring your leg higher.

My dad is telling me what to do to do better and I'm not listening like usual. He's telling how I can get my fastball faster. All I hear is blah blah blah, I just want to throw the ball hard and not be told what to do. My teammate is telling his dad what he's going to throw and his dad is giving him compliments on his accuracy. Good, that's very good, I hear his dad tell him. In between pitches I hear my dad and my teammates talk about MLB players, teams and coaches. The Tigers have a good shot going to the World Series, my dad tells another father. All I'm thinking about is throwing hard. My father tells me to start throwing the heat. I start throwing it in harder and harder. He's really throwing hard, says my teammate's dad. My dad looks at him smiling, he's proud of me. The next thing I know, my father is telling me to throw the cutter. I'm pitching the ball and right when I let go, I feel something snap in my arm. I'm done, I say, and my dad asks what happened, and I tell him and we get some ice. I think you're done with pitching, Garrett, my dad tells me, with a disappointed look on his face.

I am now in the orthopedic hospital getting x-rays to see what is wrong with my arm. I'm in a white room with a huge silver bed with a picture of Mickey Mantle on the wall. There is a computer on a desk. My father and mother are sitting and discussing what might be wrong with my arm. The doctor comes in and messes around with my arm to see where I can bend. The doctor leaves and a nurse comes and takes me to an x-ray room. It's a very small room with a metal table and a huge see-through machine hanging from the top of the wall. I sit down and the nurse makes me put my arm in positions that feel very uncomfortable,
I go back to the room where my parents are and the doctor comes in and puts my x-rays on a light. My father just came from work so he's wearing his work clothes, a button-up red shirt with khaki pants and a black belt. His hair is greased back with gel. I'm wearing

black sweats and a sweatshirt with a backwards Milwaukee cap on.
My mom's wearing her casual clothes, jeans and a zip-up . . . The
doctor tells me that I have cracked a bone in my growth plate that
holds my elbow in place.

Garrett Olson
Grade 9
Eastview High School, Apple Valley
Writer-in-residence: Laurie Lindeen

Rubbing Lotion

Here I am feeling great because
I'm petting my pitch-black dog. He feels
like dry grass. Sometimes it feels like you
just got done rubbing lotion on your
hands. He nips at the air, pretending
there is meat floating.

Jessie Hassebroek
Grade 4
Hoover Elementary School, Coon Rapids
Writer-in-residence: Susan Marie Swanson

The Window

The window is a mirror of life.
I look at it and what do I see?
Not my reflection, but the reflection of the life around me.
People, plants and animals.
Their feelings, their problems, their differences and their personality.
I see groups of black birds flying together.
I see people helping their neighbors get the cars started.
I see smoke coming out of chimneys on buildings
I see my breath when I breathe or talk when it's chilly outside.
I see all of this when I stand by the window, the mirror of life.

Iesha Abbajebel
Grade 4
Highland Park Elementary School, Saint Paul
Writer-in-residence: Nora Murphy

Listening and Dreaming

At night in the darkness
I look out the window
at all the stillness of the
world and see the crisp
yellow color of a lamp
in my neighbor's window.
Listening, listening to the
small winter breeze that
flows by. And feeling the soft
coldness of my pillow. I can
hear the floor creaking.
Then all of a sudden
I am asleep, fast asleep.
And I'm dreaming, just dreaming.

Brigette Boyer
Grade 3
South Elementary School, Saint Peter
Writer-in-residence: Susan Marie Swanson

The Catastrophic Competition

All the students were seated in the auditorium waiting for the principal to come out to announce who was going to represent the school in the athletic competition. Doing things like running, floor exercises, and things on the balance beam. I was in the back row with my best friend Kanna.

The principal came out. "The person who will be representing us is Kisa Flowright," he boomed in his loud and very superior voice. My face fell, my skin turned white. That was my name he'd called.

How could this happen to me? I thought to myself. *Why not Sue Adams, she's the best athlete in the school?* The sea of students looked just as shocked as me. The principal asked me to come to the front of the room. I hesitated and whispered the words "Oh no." I headed up, too shy to look at the crowd. Everyone knew that I was NOT a social person. The principal announced that the competition would be held at Freeman's High School two weeks from today. *Two weeks, I have two weeks to train for this, two weeks*, I thought to myself.

My best friend Kanna walked with me down the hall to where the buses were. "What am I going to do?" I asked her.

"I don't know," she answered.

"Kanna, you're a good athlete. Could you teach me how to be one too, please oh please oh pretty please," I begged her.

"Okay, okay, already," she answered. Kanna and I were next-door neighbors so it was easy to go over to each other's house. "Kisa, how about you come over tomorrow?" Kanna offered.

"Okay," I answered. Today was Friday, so tomorrow is Saturday. It was spring break too. As I walked up my driveway, I thought to myself, "I'm doomed."

When I got in my house I said hi to my mom and headed up to my room. My cat Kyo was waiting for me there. I looked at myself in the mirror. "Not much," I thought aloud. I saw long black hair, always in two equal braids. I always wore blue jeans, and wore a regular tank top. I told Kyo about all my troubles. How I have to represent the school in an athletic competition, and how I have to train twenty times harder than anyone else in the competition just so I won't make a fool of myself.

"Mom, I'm doomed," is what I said when I came downstairs.

"Why?" she asked.

"Because I have to represent the school in an athletic competition."

"That sounds great!" she exclaimed. Mom didn't seem to get that I am not the athletic kind of person.

"When's Dad going to come home?" I asked.

"He'll probably be home at six o'clock."

Well, I might as well get some of my chores over with, I thought to myself. I rode my horses once in awhile, but not much.

The next day I woke up. "Okay Kisa, today is the day," I said aloud. I got dressed and ate breakfast. "Mom, I'm heading over to Kanna's house now, okay?" I said.

"Um, okay," she answered, in her distant morning voice.

I knocked on Kanna's door. "I'm here," I said when she opened the door.

"Hey Kisa, good morning," she replied. Her home was so neat and clean that it was frightening. "Okay, today we'll start by running around the block for a few hours," she said in a confident voice.

"What!?" I was shocked.

"W-E A-R-E G-O-I-N-G O-N A R-U-N," she spelled out in a sarcastic voice. You didn't have to spell it out for me, you know. We started out on our run. Kanna could last for hours running without even breaking a sweat. I was gone in the first ten minutes. "Come on Kisa, you can do it," she said encouragingly.

"Dying," I panted. We ran for two whole hours!

My legs hurt so much the next day. "Okay, now what?" I asked.

"Well, we could do floor exercises or start on the balance beam or more running," she offered.

Let's see running, hard; balance beam, no way; gymnastics, impossible, but floor exercises aren't that bad, I thought to myself. "Floor exercises," I answered. We headed over to the school so we could practice.

I was actually catching on to a bunch of the things that I was practicing. Jess walked in the door just as I was getting the hang of flips, with Sue Adams, the best athlete in the school. The most athletic person in school was here to mock me or help me. I didn't know which. It was definitely mock. She criticized how I did it and then showed off. I guess she was still mad that I had won the award and not her. It wasn't exactly like an award to me, more like a punishment. After Sue was done mocking me, which wasn't until thirty minutes later, we started practicing again.

"So what are the different things that I have to do in the competition?" I asked Kanna.

"The principal explained that when he announced that you were going to represent the school in the competition."

"I guess I was in a bit of a daze."

"You have to run two miles, do a program using your floor exercises, and a few tricks on the balance beam," Kanna answered.

I had really gotten the hang of floor exercises. I was now reasonably good at cartwheels, sit-ups, handstands, flips, and walking on my hands.

"Wow, you've improved a lot in the last two days, Kisa!" Kanna exclaimed.

One week had passed since my first day practicing for the competition. I was really getting the hang of running, floor exercises and the balance beam. In school, we had just started working in gymnastics. Marsha Baker took gymnastics. Marsha Baker was a stuck-up girl with blonde hair and electric blue eyes. She always wore mini skirts and halter-tops with high heels; she also wore way too much makeup and jewelry. Marsha had a talent for judging people before she even knew them. Marsha was also a know-it-all. The first time I saw her, she flung her snooty nose as high in the air as possible. She had ignored me ever since.

Gym class came. "Well, I guess I should try gymnastics," I said aloud. Our gym teacher Mr. Tezuka lined us all up in front of the balance beam.

First, we all walked across the beam. Then we skipped across the beam. Next we walked across the beam on our hands. Last, we did a flip in the middle of the beam. This was for the students who took gymnastics or had a very big interest in it. Marsha had aced every single task Mr. Tezuka had given her. So did Sue. I was all right, I guess. Okay, now I knew that I was ready for the competition. I had six more days to master all of the skills that I had learned in the last eight days.

It was now the day of the competition. I was so nervous that you could have seen me shaking from a mile away. First was the balance beam. The first person who went, thankfully was not me. In fact, I wasn't the second, third or fourth, I was last. I had seen so many great performances that I had high expectations.

Okay, just calm down, I thought to myself.

"You can do it Kisa," Kanna yelled out from somewhere in the crowd. I started by running across the beam. I did a cartwheel, then a flip with a perfect landing. Everybody cheered for me It felt great!

Next was my floor exercise program. This time I was first. I did my program to some hip-hop music. I did five cartwheels in a row. Then I did a flip, then another. I did some back bends too. It ended in the splits. The next and final part was the 2 mile race. We had two hours before the race to get ready. Every day for two weeks I had gone on a two hour run with Kanna.

"That better pay off," I thought aloud. We had what basically looked like a baseball diamond to run around. We had to run around the diamond two and a half times. "Oh no," I whispered under my breath as we all lined up to start the race. The whistle blew and my legs took over. I started out running moderately fast and I was at my fastest when I saw the finish line. I came in first but only just. The whole school was there to cheer for me. Even Sue and Marsha cheered.

I, Kisa Flowright, the girl who was very shy and non-social, just won an athletic competition. I couldn't help but think that only two weeks ago I had hated sports and trying to be social. Now I had won this trophy in front of tons of people. I'm glad now that I was chosen to represent the school. My school got a trophy bigger than I am! After the competition, I was much better in gym, and tried harder on the things I was not familiar with. I was also more of a social person after the competition and not as shy. Now Sue and Marsha are my friends, I have lots more friends now. Yay!

Ayla Rubenstein
Grade 5
Afton-Lakeland Elementary School, Lakeland
Writer-in-residence: Stephen Peters

Flecks of Paint on a Desert Canvas

I trudge through the vast abyss of desert,
Sand is being picked up by the fierce, raging winds,
The dry smell of sand shoots up my nostrils as I attempt to take a
breath,
I close my eyes against the grains of sand assaulting me,
I shield my face with a forearm for a moment, then open my eyes.
The world is dark.
I glance around, realizing that the darkness was just a shadow,
Ruins of an ancient city loom over me,
Not threatening, but . . .
Defeated?
Splotches of red, dancing across smooth, sand-worn walls catch my
eye.
Blood.
I wander farther into the relic city,
Discovering things . . .
a spear here, a broken vase there,

Aftereffects of war.
I inspect broken houses, fallen carts, a disheveled temple, and other
various things.
I
muse silently to myself,
Could this ever happen to me? Where I live? I imagine a snow-cov-
ered landscape,
empty broken homes, aflame around me, screams echoing off the
pavement.
I shake my head violently, banishing the thoughts from my head,
I continue onward,
Even though I'm trying my hardest, I can still feel the gears in my
head turning.
The blood and sand splayed across buildings form pictures,
The desert, flying around me, its own living canvas,
I sit down in the middle of an old street as vivid bursts of creativity
pulsate through
my
mind.

I am inspired
I take out my notebook and begin to write.

Lacey O'Leary
Grade 8
Falcon Ridge Middle School, Apple Valley
Writer-in-residence: Diego Vázquez

I Could've Died

It was the end of a long tiring day. Not a particularly good one either. I was so tired I couldn't keep my eyes open. I leaned my head against the window of our car as rain slowly tapped against it. All of the voices and sounds of the road just kind of faded away. All of a sudden I heard my mom scream. There was a loud bang and a jolt and the seatbelt cut sharply into my neck as we skidded across the intersection. My glasses flew off and my mind went blank.

"Is everybody okay?" I heard my mom in the front seat.

"Oh man, where are my glasses?" I replied.

My sister handed me my glasses off the floor and we pulled to the side of the road.

What the hell just happened? I thought rubbing my neck. My mind a blank, I was in shock. It's amazing what can happen in five seconds.

I noticed another car stopped on the cement section that divided the two sides of the road. That's when it registered. *Car crash. I was just in a car crash. I could have died.* I sat there dumbly as the thought ran through my mind over and over. *Could have died. Could have died. Could have died.*

"Oh, my God. Is everyone all right?" It was a Palestinian woman with a thick accent, the driver of the other car. "That was all my fault. I am so sorry." Her kids stood under a red-and-white striped umbrella. *No one's hurt. That's good.* It's a funny feeling, shock. Your mind is totally clear and rational but at the same time you feel as if you couldn't add two and two to save your life. My mom broke the silence.

"Nobody's hurt?" she asked. "You're sure?" *Poor mom. Brand new car and everything. Doesn't even have the new plates on yet and here it is all smashed up.* The front end was smashed and fluids were leaking out. She had only had it a week and it wasn't even drivable anymore.

"No," I replied finally, "I'm okay." The seat belt had dug into my neck at impact leaving a red line. I had had worse cat scratches.

A few minutes later a policeman came to get our side of the story. He took down our names and told my mom to move to the back seat. The airbags hadn't gone off during the accident, but he said they could go off at any moment. So we sat in the back seat— my mom, sister, and me—all listening to the rain pouring down.

Half an hour later the cop said we could go home. We crammed into the back of the police car. It's strange to see the world through barred windows. I could see the road slick with rainwater, smooth and black, making it look like a dark river.

Although only an hour had passed, it was all very dreamlike. It was as if it had happened to someone else. Then the worst thought of all popped into my mind. *I have a paper, a math test and a vocabulary quiz tomorrow.* With a groan I slid down farther into my seat.

When we finally got home we all tried to act as normal as possible. I could tell that everyone was pretty shaken up. We were all twitchy and talking very slowly as if we were trying to make up for time speeding up the moment of the crash by talking slower than normal.

My sister and I, having nothing better to do, began to do the dishes. It's surprising how comforting chores can be. It's as if you want to convince yourself that nothing out of the ordinary has happened. We unloaded the dishwasher and did the dishes without being told. With the dishes done I sat down, geometry book open on my lap, trying to study. I stared blankly at the list of chapter vocabulary for several long minutes before closing the book and cramming it back into my backpack.

The pizza we ordered arrived. I sat down at our familiar old kitchen table, running my finger along the various scratches on the table, along the stain left by my hair dye, remembering every time I had sat there. I slowly finished my pizza. *Well, no one can say today was boring.* Smirking, I left the table to go write my memoir.

Teagan Riehle
Grade 9
Eastview High School, Apple Valley
Writer-in-residence: Laurie Lindeen

A Favor for Papa

My grandfather's funeral. Bowed heads, casket, crowded, cold. My father stands with his brother. My mother and brother save us a seat in the front pew. Family and friends offer us their sympathy. We sit in the church. The tall roof is high above us. I am eight and unable to take the tension and sorrow any longer. I go and stand outside alone, and fight the tears that threaten to come pouring out. I cannot cry, I cannot make my father sad.

I stand in the church garden. The leaves of the plants are covered in a light frost. I lean against the cold brick wall of the church. I take five deep breaths and re-enter the church through the heavy glass doors. Inside is a small hallway running the length of the church. Some of my relatives (at least I think they're my relatives, heck, they could be random people from off the street for all I know) are looking at a table full of brochures. I suspect they were just trying to give their eyes something to do other than crying. I try it, but it doesn't work. Then I walk into the actual church in search of my mother. The roof is extremely high; all of the windows are stained with enchanting pictures of Jesus, Mary, and the angels. As soon as I look lower, I bolt out of the room. I had seen it. There to the right of the door was a beautifully polished wooden casket on a set of wheels. It was half open. I didn't see the body, but just knowing there was a body in the casket was enough to scare me out of my wits. I notice that I'd dropped my purse near the casket, but I wasn't about to go get it by myself.

I find my dad and tell him about the purse. "You better go get it," he says.

"I can't," I reply.

"Why not?"

"It's next to grandpa, I'm too scared."

"I'll go with you in a sec."

I hesitate at the door. "Come on," my dad said. I hold my breath and enter. Dad grabs my purse and stands with Nana, my brother Tim, and Mom around the casket looking at Papa. I have a strange urge to look at him. Dad signals me to come over, and I oblige. I look in the casket. I thought he would be green and decaying, but he just looked like he was sleeping. (Never trust Tim Burton movies.) It made me happy to see how peaceful he looked. We stood around him saying the Our Father. Suddenly Nana reaches out to touch Papa's belly.

"Oh Nana, don't," I say. Too late. She has her hand on him and is talking to him.

"I love you Howard. Good-bye," she says to Papa's body. She pushes on his stomach lightly and a small burst of air escapes from his throat. I jump five feet into the last pew. Luckily my scream comes out as a quiet squeal. My family turns and laughs at me.

"He breathed," I say, still shocked.

"He just had some extra air in his lungs that came out when Nana pushed on his chest," Dad explains, "Are you okay?"

"I'm fine!"

That is a lie. I am far from fine. Papa is dead. Just yesterday he was there. He may not have been able to open his eyes and talk, but he was there. Now he's gone forever.

The next day we go to Papa's favorite place, Artist's Point. Dad is carrying Papa's ashes. We get to the point and scatter the ashes in Lake Superior. We all say a silent prayer. Once we get back to the beach, I begin to cry again. I feel like I don't have a connection to Papa anymore. Papa's dog Mickey comes over to see me. I reach out to pet him. I cry harder. Mickey was Papa's life (aside from Nana, of course). Mickey was human to Papa; he even gave Mickey human food for dinner. I laugh at that memory. Mickey was going to the dog kennel today to live, which made me very sad.

"Come here Elizabeth, we need to talk to you," my parents called to me.

"Okay," I say and run over.

"Do you think you're ready for a big responsibility?" they ask.

"Yes."

"Papa wanted you to have Mickey."

I stare at them dumbfounded. Even though I am only eight, I understand what this means. Papa wanted me to have one of his most precious possessions. I beam at their burred faces through my tears, and at that moment I can feel Papa smiling down on me.

Liz Massie
Grade 9
Eastview High School, Apple Valley
Writer-in-residence: Laurie Lindeen

Nursing Home

A nursing home. Weird smelling, cold air, identical rooms, and old people. Gloria is sitting at her table complaining about today's cheddar and potato soup. Bill is sitting with his hat and glasses that he wears every day. And Ruth in her room with her computer that she barely ever leaves. I look around the social room; I smell weird air—it smells like old people. I see the birdcage and the lady that sits there all day every day. I try not to laugh while talking to Bill. I smile as Gloria tells me her life story and I try to figure out what to say when I'm with Ruth. I am thirteen and in a nursing home in Rapid City, South Dakota for a week of my summer. I organize Ruth's envelopes, listen to Gloria, and laugh with Bill. Wash your hands after touching any wheelchair or elderly person.

Bill was the first person I talked to. He was in his early eighties, I'll bet. He wore a cool hat and glasses and his Coca-Cola pajamas. He greeted me with a "Hello, I'm Bill. And who are you?" and a firm handshake. Bill and I talked for a long time about a bunch of stuff. I looked to his right and saw his walker while he was telling me about riding his bike down a big hill. I laughed because I knew he was lying. A few minutes later he said, "Yep, I own this place. I bought it about six years ago." Another lie. Bill told me stories about his crazy life and his two daughters that he adopted. Bill said that his two daughters were coming to pick him up for the fourth of July. It was the third of July when I talked to him. We came back the next day and I saw Bill sitting in the exact same place. I went over and asked, "Bill, why aren't you out with your daughters?" He replied, "Do I know you? Well, I'm Bill." It was then that I realized that Bill had Alzheimer's.

Then I met Gloria. She was there when I first walked into the nursing home, sitting there in her pink cat sweater, which was way too big for her stick-skinny body. I started talking to Gloria after I was done talking to Bill. She kept saying what a "cutie" I was and how she had a grandson my age and how she would love it if we met. One of the nurses told me that Gloria had had brain surgery earlier in the year and that she probably wouldn't remember me the next day. When it was time to go I said, "Bye Gloria, see you tomorrow." She said back, "See ya, kiddo, I can't wait to see you tomorrow." I thought to myself that it was too bad that she won't remember me. The next day I went over to Gloria and before I even introduced myself she said, "Do I know you? You look very familiar." I introduced myself again. There I listened to her whole life story again. At the end of our conversation she asked me if I would like to go out back. I willingly helped her walk with her cane out to the back, but didn't know she was headed to the smoking house out back. She asked me if I want to have a smoke. I ran and got a nurse so she could deal with it.

The next person I met was an amazing lady named Ruth. I walked into a room that was identical to everyone else's. I saw a bigger lady in a wheelchair sitting at her computer. I was sent to Ruth's room because she is paralyzed from the waist down and can barely move her arms and she needed someone to put stamps on her envelopes. The amazing thing about Ruth is that she is writing a book. I walked in and saw stacks of boxes and books. I saw a computer on a table and Ruth in front of the computer. Her computer doesn't have a keyboard only a headset so Ruth can type by talking out her book. I think the only time I saw her move her hands was when she was pointing to where the smiley-faced stamps were or when she lifted her water bottle with a super long straw to her mouth. The first thing she said to me was, "Don't call me 'hon,' 'sweetie,' or 'honey.' I have a name and it's Ruth; I expect you to respect that." I did. Ruth taught me a lot and she made her opinions loud and clear. Her book was about women's rights and how they have changed over the years. I don't think I'll ever get around to reading her book, but I hold the highest respect for Ruth.

A nursing home. Weird smelling, cold air, identical rooms, and old people. Bill, Gloria, and Ruth. Yes, I think I spent one week of my summer with the right people in the right place.

Sally Fifield
Grade 9
Eastview High School, Apple Valley
Writer-in-residence: Laurie Lindeen

Angels

I hear the angels
singing
I look down
the grass is shivering

Forrest Ahrens
Grade 1
St. Anthony Park Elementary School, Saint Paul
Writer-in-residence: John Minczeski

Krupp, Anna Lucia Pax	Blake Middle School	41
Kuemmel, Meghan	Grey Cloud Elementary School	65
Lonergan, Jared	Lake Junior High School	49
Massie, Liz	Eastview High School	114
McCauley, Tata	Patrick Henry High School	47
Mclean, Taj	Webster Magnet School	34
Metzger, Kellie	Falcon Ridge Middle School	82
Minnihan, Serena	Gatewood Elementary School	17
Mohamed, Fadli	Ubah Medical Academy	33
Murphy, Chris	Bailey Elementary School	77
Nelson, Kyle	Royal Oaks Elementary School	21
Nguyen, Lyly	Columbia Heights High School	35
O'Callaghan, Abby	Glen Lake Elementary School	76
O'Leary, Lacey	Falcon Ridge Middle School	110
Olson, Garrett	Eastview High School	101
Park, Do-Hyoung	Interdistrict Downtown School	99
Pearce's Class, Ms.	North Intermediate School	36
Pietraszewski, Hailey	Madison Elementary School	52
Poepping, Lauren	Rice Elementary School	68
Poole, Chole	Patrick Henry High School	73
Raygor, Logan	Oak Hill Community School	44
Reichert, Marty	Eastview High School	45
Riehle, Teagan	Eastview High School	112
Rigstad, Elizabeth	Roseau Secondary School	12
Roeun, Saray	Hazel Park Middle School	43
Ross's Class, Ms.	Dayton Elementary School	27
Rowlison, Mykaelah	Middleton Elementary School	39
Rubenstein, Ayla	Afton-Lakeland Elementary School	106
Schnabel's Class, Ms.	Riverview Specialty School	91
Schumacher, George	Patrick Henry High School	54
Scott, Curtesa	Webster Magnet School	38
Shavers, Yahrielle	Liberty Ridge Elementary School	20
Stroot, Jaylin	Roseau Secondary School	32
Stuckey, James	Hazel Park Middle School	74
Vang, Tyler	Rondo Community Outreach Library	48
Weldon, Paige	LeSueur-Henderson Middle School	64

Index by School

Katherine Curren Elementary School	Michelle Atwood	98
Lake Junior High School	Jared Lonergan	49
LeSueur-Henderson Middle School	Paige Weldon	64
Liberty Ridge Elementary School	Matthew Ickstadt	24
Liberty Ridge Elementary School	Yahrielle Shavers	20
Lindbergh Elementary School	Ms. Dawson & Mrs. Geyer's Class	86
Madison Elementary School	Hailey Pietraszewski	52
Meadowbrook Elementary School	Ruby Joy Kinney	92
Meadowbrook Elementary School	Justin Brown	84
Mendota Elementary School	Madeline Hudalla	88
Mendota Elementary School	Sage Gegelman	85
Mendota Elementary School	Jamie Herridge	83
Middleton Elementary School	Mykaelah Rowlison	39
Normandale French Immersion School	Julia Brooks	58
North Intermediate School	Ms. Pearce's Class	36
Oak Hill Community School	Amelia Broman	62
Oak Hill Community School	Logan Raygor	44
Oak Hill Montessori	Daniel Johnson	28
Park Elementary School	Taylor Kiemele	60
Patrick Henry High School	Tata McCauley	47
Patrick Henry High School	Chole Poole	73
Patrick Henry High School	George Schumacher	54
Rice Elementary School	Mitchell Zabel	55
Rice Elementary School	Lauren Poepping	68
Riverview Specialty School	Ms. Schnabel's Class	91
Roseau Secondary School	Elizabeth Rigstad	12
Roseau Secondary School	Katie Hoff	59
Roseau Secondary School	Jaylin Stroot	32
Royal Oaks Elementary School	Kyle Nelson	21
South Elementary School	Brigette Boyer	105
St. Anthony Park Elementary School	Forrest Ahrens	118
St. Anthony Park Elementary School	Madeleine Hamerski	37
St. Joseph's School	Ellie Wolfe	71

Program Writers
2006-2007

Kelly Regan Barnhill

Lisa Bullard

Sarah Fox

Dana Jensen

Tou SaiKo Lee

Laurie Lindeen

Charlie Maguire

John Minczeski

Nora Murphy

Rachel Nelson

Marie Olofsdotter

Stephen Peters

Joyce Sidman

Julia Klatt Singer

Susan Marie Swanson

Diego Vázquez

THE LILLIAN WRIGHT AWARDS FOR CREATIVE WRITING

ℰℭ ℭℬ

These awards are intended to recognize the finest literary achievements among young writers in Minnesota. The Wright Awards are underwritten by the Lillian Wright and C. Emil Berglund Foundation. Award winners from **EYES FULL OF SKY** are formally honored at the December 2007 Publication Celebration.

COMPAS is proud to honor the winners of the fourteenth annual Lillian Wright Awards for Creative Writing, given to the best examples of student writing featured in the 2006-2007 COMPAS Writers & Artists in the Schools anthology, **EYES FULL OF SKY**. The 2006-2007 winners are:

Best Writing in Grades K-3: "Pencil's Life Cycle," by Abby O'Callaghan, Grade 2, Glen Lake Elementary School, Hopkins

Best Prose in Grades 4-6: "Life Goes On," by Do-Hyoung Park, Grade 4, Interdistrict Downtown School, Minneapolis

Best Poetry in Grades 4-6: "Unearthed Feelings," by Franchesca Castro, Grade 5, Alice Smith Elementary School, Hopkins

Judge's Choice in Grades 4-6: "Brownies," by Kyle Nelson, Grade 5, Royal Oaks Elementary School, Woodbury

Best Poetry in Grades 7-8: "My Town," by Jaylin Stroot, Grade 8, Roseau Secondary School, Roseau

Best Prose in Grades 7-12: "I Could've Died," by Teagan Reihle, Grade 9, Eastview High School, Apple Valley

Best Poetry in Grades 9-12: "Another Family," by Lyly Nguyen, Grade 9, Columbia Heights High School, Columbia Heights

Best Song: "Rolling to be a Champion," by Ms. Wilson's Varsity Choir, Grades 9-12, Cloquet High School, Cloquet

Awards Judge: LaRae Ludwig is a longtime contact teacher for WAITS at LeSueur-Henderson Middle School. She teaches Grade 7.

Writers & Artists in the Schools
Anthology Order Form
Tear out or copy this form and return it with your payment

Name:_____

School/Organization:_____

Address:_____

Phone number/E-mail: _____

Quantity	Year	Title	Price
_____	2007	Eyes Full of Sky	12.00
_____	2006	The Wind Tells Me Stories	12.00
_____	2005	My Mind Can See in the Night	12.00
_____	2004	Sing to the Dust	12.00
_____	2003	In My Hand Forever	12.00
_____	2002	Good Morning Tulip	12.00
_____	2001	Northern Lights	10.00
_____	2000	Give Me Your Hand	10.00
_____	1999	I Stand on You and Sing That Song	9.00
_____	1998	River Pigs	9.00
_____	1997	A Special Stretch of Sky	9.00
_____	1996	Rooftop Jailbirds	8.00
_____	1995	Oh, Light Sleeper, Wild Dreamer	8.00
_____	1994	The Dream of the Whale	8.00
_____	1993	Come Home Before Dark	8.00
_____	1992	If You Praise a Word, It Turns into a Poem	8.00

Earlier issues are also available, please call for information!

_____ Class Set (min. 10 copies of each book) at 25% discount

_____ Total cost of books ordered

_____ Minnesota Sales Tax (7%)

_____ Postage and handling *($2 first book, $1 each additional book)*

_____ *I would like to make a tax deductible donation to COMPAS!*

_____ **TOTAL DUE**

Please make checks payable to COMPAS
Mail orders to: COMPAS, 75 West 5th Street, #304, St. Paul, MN 55102

Your support allows us to continue offering affordable programs to schools throughout Minnesota! Thank you.